THE MOSQUITO FLEET

BERN KEATING

SBS SCHOLASTIC BOOK SERVICES
New York Toronto London Auckland Sydney

To Lieut. Commander Brinkley Bass and Lieut. Commander Clyde Hopkins McCroskey, Jr., who gallantly gave their lives during World War II. They were brave seamen and good friends.

Photographs used on the cover are courtesy of the U.S. Navy.

 This edition is published by Scholastic Book Services, a division of Scholastic Magazines, Inc., by arrangement with G. P. Putnam's Sons.

3rd printing November 1968 Printed in the U.S.A.

CONTENTS

HISTORICAL MATERIAL in this book comes from action reports, squadron histories, and other naval records on file at the historical records section in Arlington, Va. Most valuable was the comprehensive history of PT actions written by Commodore Robert Bulkley for the Navy. The Bulkley history was in manuscript form at the time I did research for this book. The broad outline of naval history comes mostly from the *History of U. S. Naval Operations in World War II* of Samuel Eliot Morison. I am grateful to several PT veterans for their generous contribution of diaries, letters, anecdotes, etc., which have been drawn on for human interest material. Among these kind correspondents are: James Cunningham of Shreveport, La., Roger Jones of Nassau, Bahama Islands, Lieut. Commander R. W. Brown of Scituate, Mass., Capt. Stanley Barnes of the War College, Carlisle Barracks, Pa., James Newberry of Memphis, Tenn., and Arthur Murray Preston, of Washington, D. C. The officers of Peter Tare Inc., a PT veterans organization, have been helpful.

1.

The First PTs:

Facts and Fictions

IN MARCH 17, 1942, General Douglas MacArthur arrived safely in Australia after a flight from his doomed army in the Philippine Islands. The people of America, staggering from three months of unrelieved disaster, felt a tremendous lift of spirits.

America needed a lift of spirits.

Three months before, without the formality of declaring war, Japan had sneaked a fleet of planes from a carrier force into the main American naval base at Pearl Harbor in Hawaii, and in one Sunday morning's work the planes had smashed America's Pacific battle line under a shower of bombs and torpedoes. Without a fighting fleet, America had been helpless to stop the swift spread of the Japanese around the far shores and islands of the Pacific basin.

Guam and Wake Island had been overrun; Manila, Hong Kong, Singapore, the East Indies, had been gobbled up. Our fighting sailors, until the disaster of the sneak attack on Pearl Harbor, had been boasting around the navy clubs that the American fleet could sail up one side of the Japanese homeland and down the other side, shooting holes in the islands and watching them sink from sight. Now they ground their teeth in humiliation and rage, unable to get at the Japanese because the Pacific Fleet battle line lay in the ooze on the bottom of Pearl Harbor. His Imperial Japanese Majesty's navy was steaming, virtually unopposed, wherever its infuriatingly cocky admirals willed.

When a combined Dutch-American flotilla had tried to block the Japanese landings on Java, the Allied navies had promptly lost 13 of their pitifully few remaining destroyers and cruisers—and the tragic sacrifice had not even held up the Japanese advance for more than a few hours.

The naval officers of the Allies had had to make a painful change in their opinion of the Japanese sailor's ability; he had turned out to be a formidable fighting man.

On land, the Japanese army was even more spectacularly competent. Years of secret training in island-hopping and jungle warfare had paid off for the Japanese. With frightening ease, they had brushed aside opposition everywhere—everywhere, that is, except in the Philippine Islands, where General MacArthur's outnumbered and underequipped Filipino and American fighters had improvised a savage resistance; had patched together a kind of Hooligan's Army, fleshing out the thin ranks of the defenders with headquarters clerks and ship's cooks, with electrician's mates and chaplain's assistants, with boatless boatswain's mates and planeless pilots.

MacArthur's patchwork army had harried the Japanese advance and had stubbornly fought a long retreat down the Island of Luzon. It was bottled up on the Bataan Peninsula and on the island fortress of Corregidor in Manila Bay, and it was already doomed, everybody knew that. The flight of its commanding general only emphasized that it had been written off, but the tremendous fight it was putting up had salved every American's wounded national pride. Besides, the very fact that MacArthur had been ordered out of the islands clearly meant that America was going back, once the nation had caught its breath and recovered from Pearl Harbor.

General MacArthur, with a talent for flamboyant leadership that amounted to genius of a sort, emitted the sonorous phrase: "I shall return."

A few sour critics, immune to the MacArthur charm, deplored his use of the first person singular when the first person plural would have been more graceful—and more accurate—but the phrase caught on in the free world.

"I shall return." The phrase promised brave times ahead, when the galling need to retreat would end and America would begin the journey back to Bataan.

A stirring prospect, but what a long journey it was going to be. The most ignorant could look at a map and see that MacArthur's return trip was going to take years. And yet his trip out had taken only days. A few of the curious wondered how his escape had been engineered. News stories said that MacArthur had flown into Australia. But where had he found a plane? For days America had been told that on the shrinking Luzon beachhead no airstrips remained in American hands. Where had MacArthur gone to find a friendly airfield, and how had he gone there through the swarming patrols of the Japanese naval blockade?

The full story of MacArthur's escape, when it was told, became one of the top adventure stories of World War II.

First came the bare announcement that it was on a motor torpedo boat — a PT boat in Navy parlance, and a mosquito boat in journalese—that the general had made the first leg of his flight across enemy-infested seas. Then a crack journalist named William L. White interviewed the officers of the PT rescue squadron and wrote a book about the escape and about the days when the entire American naval striking force in the Philippines had shrunk to six, then four, then three, then one of the barnacle-encrusted plywood motorboats hardly bigger than a stockbroker's cabin cruiser.

The book was called *They Were Expendable,* and it became a runaway best-seller. It was condensed for *Reader's Digest* and featured in *Life* Magazine, and it made the PT sailor the glamour boy of America's surface fleet. *They Were Expendable* makes exciting reading today, but the book's success spawned a swarm of magazine and newspaper articles about the PT navy, and some of them were distressingly irresponsible. Quite innocently, William White himself added to the PT's exaggerated reputation for being able to lick all comers, regardless of size. He wrote his book in wartime and so had no way of checking the squadron's claims of torpedo successes. Naturally, as any generous reporter would have done, he gave full credit to its claims of an amazing bag – two light cruisers, two transports and an oil tanker, besides enemy barges, landing craft and planes.

Postwar study of Japanese naval archives shows no evidence that any Japanese ships were torpedoed at the times and places the Squadron Three sailors claim to have hit them. Of course, airplane and PT pilots are notoriously overoptimistic – they have to be optimistic by nature even to get into the cockpits of their frail craft and set out for combat. And yet any realistic person who has worked in government archives hesitates to give full weight to a damage assessment by an office research clerk as opposed to the evidence of combat eyewitnesses.

Postwar evaluation specialists would not confirm the sinking of a 5,000-ton armed merchant vessel at Binanga on January 19, 1942, but Army observers on Mount Mariveles watched through 20-power glasses as a ship sank, and they reported even the number and caliber of the guns in its armament.

On February 2, 1942, Army lookouts reported that a badly crippled cruiser was run aground (and later cut up for scrap) at the right time and place to be the cruiser claimed by PT 32. Evaluation clerks could not find a record of this ship sinking either, so the PT claim is denied.

Unfortunately, the most elaborately detailed claim of all, the sinking of a *Kuma* class cruiser off Cebu Island by PTs 34 and 41, most certainly is not valid, because the cruiser itself sent a full report of the battle to Japanese Navy headquarters and admitted being struck by one dud torpedo (so much at least of the PT claim is true), but the cruiser, which happened to be the *Kuma* itself, was undamaged and survived to be sunk by a British submarine late in the war.

The undeniable triumph of Squadron Three was the flight of MacArthur. On March 11, 1942, at Corregidor, the four surviving boats of the squadron picked up the general, his staff and selected officers and technicians, the general's wife and son and — most astonishingly — a Chinese nurse for the four-year-old boy. In a series of night dashes from island to island through Japanese-infested seas, the little flotilla carried the escaping brass to the island of Mindanao, where the generals and admirals caught a B 17 Flying Fortress bomber flight for Australia.

The fantastic and undeniably exaggerated claims of sinkings are regrettable, but in no way detract from the bravery of the sailors of Squadron Three. They were merely the victims of the nation's desperate need for victories.

William White's contribution to the false giant-killer image of the PTs is understandable, but other correspondents were less responsible. One, famous and highly respected, said that all PTs were armed with three-inch cannon. Putting such a massive weapon on the fragile plywood deck of a PT boat was a bit like arming a four-year-old boy with a big-league baseball bat – it's just too much weapon for such a little fellow to carry. The same reckless writer said that PT boats cruised at 70 knots. Another said that a PT could pace a new car – which amounts to another claim for a 70-knot speed. Almost all of the reporters, some of whom surely knew better, wrote about the PTs' armament as though the little boats could slug it out with ships of the line.

In the fantasies spun by the nation's press, the PTs literally ran rings around enemy destroyers and socked so many torpedoes into Japanese warships that you almost felt sorry for the outclassed and floundering enemy.

PT sailors read these romances and gritted their teeth. They knew too painfully well that the stories were not true.

What was the truth about the PT?

Early in World War II, before the Japanese attack on Pearl Harbor pulled the United States into the war then raging in Europe against Germany and Italy and in China against Japan, the American Navy had been tinkering around with various designs of fast small boats armed with torpedoes. British coastal forces had been making good use of small, fast torpedo boats, and the American Navy borrowed much from British designs.

On July 24, 1941 – four and a half months before America entered the war – the Navy held the Plywood Derby, a test speed run of experimental PTs in the open Atlantic off Long Island. The course ran around the east end of Block Island, around the Fire Island lightship to a finish line at Montauk Point Whistling Buoy. Two PTs of the Elco design finished with best average speeds – 39.72 and 37.01 knots – but boats of other designs had smaller turning circles. Over a measured mile the Elcos did 45.3 knots with a light load and 44.1 knots with a heavy load.

On a second Plywood Derby, the Elcos raced against the destroyer *Wilkes*. Seas were running eight feet high – in one stretch the destroyer skipper reported 15-foot waves – and the little cockleshells took a terrible beating. Most of the time they were out of sight in the trough of the seas or hidden by flying spray. The destroyer won the race, but the Navy board had been impressed by the seaworthiness of the tough little boats, and the Navy decided to go ahead with a torpedo-boat program. The board standardized on the 80-foot Elco and the 78-foot Higgins designs, and the boatyards fell to work.

The boats were built of layers of plywood. Draft to the tips of the propellers was held to a shallow five feet six inches, so that the PT could sneak close to an enemy beach on occasion as a kind of seagoing cavalry, to do dirty work literally at the crossroads.

Three Packard V-12 engines gave a 4,500-shaft horsepower and drove the boats, under ideal conditions, as fast as 45 knots – but conditions were seldom ideal. A PT in the battle zone was almost never in top racing form. In action the PT was usually overloaded, was often running on jury-rig repairs and spare parts held together with adhesive tape and ingenuity. In tropic waters the hull was soon sporting a long, green beard of water plants that could cut the PT's speed in half. Many of the PTs that fought the bloody battles that follow in these pages were doing well to hit 29 or even 27 knots.

The American Navy had learned the hard way that any enemy destroyer could make 35 knots, and many of them could do considerably better — plenty fast enough to run down a PT boat, especially after a few months of action had cut the PT's speed.

The normal boat crew was three officers and 14 men, though the complement varied widely under combat conditions. The boat carried enough provisions for about five days.

As for that bristling armament the correspondents talked about, a PT boat originally carried four torpedoes and tubes, and two 50-caliber twin machine-gun mounts. In combat PT skippers improvised installation of additional weapons, and by the war's end all boats had added some combination of 40-mm. autocannon, 37-mm. cannon, 20-mm. antiaircraft autocannon, rocket launchers, and 60-mm. mortars. In some zones they even discarded the torpedoes and added still more automatic weapons, to give themselves heavier broadsides for duels with armed enemy small craft.

Pound for pound, the PT boat was by far the most heavily armed vessel afloat, but that does not mean that a PT flyweight, no matter how tough for its size, was a match for an enemy heavyweight. PT sailors never hesitated to tackle an enemy destroyer, but they knew that a torpedo boat could stand up to an all-out brawl with an alert and aroused destroyer the way a spunky rat terrier can stand up to a hungry wolf. After all, the full and proper name of a destroyer is *torpedo-boat* destroyer.

The PT's main tactic was not the hell-roaring dash of the correspondents' romances, but a sneaky, quiet approach in darkness or fog. The PT was designed to slip slowly and quietly into an enemy formation in bad visibility, to fire torpedoes at the handiest target, and to escape behind a smoke screen with whatever speed the condition of the boat permitted. With luck, the screening destroyers would lose the PT in the smoke, the confusion, and the darkness. Without luck – well, in warfare everybody has to take some chances.

What most annoyed the PT sailors about their lurid press was that the truth made an even better story. After all, they argued, it takes guts to ease along at night in an agonizingly slow approach to an enemy warship that will chew you to bloody splinters if the lookouts ever spot you. And it takes real courage to bore on into slingshot range when you know that the enemy can easily run you down if your torpedoes miss or fail to explode, as they did all too often. Compared to this reality, one of those imaginary 70-knot blitzes would be a breeze.

One disgusted PT sailor wrote: "Publicity has reached the point where glorified stories are not genuinely flattering. Most PT men resent the wild, fanciful tales that tend to belittle their real experience. . . . There is actually little glamour for a PT. The excitement of battle is tempered by many dull days of inactivity, long nights of fruitless patrol, and dreary hours of foul weather at sea in a small boat."

He griped that the PT sailor would prefer the tribute of "They were dependable" to "They were expendable."

Maybe so, but the public just would not have it that way. The dash and audacity of the sailors of those little boats had appealed to the American mind. It was the story of David and Goliath again, and the sailors in the slingshot navy, no matter how they balked, joined the other wild and woolly heroes of legend who go joyously into battle against giants.

This is the story of what the mosquito fleet really did.

2.

Attrition at Guadalcanal

IN AUGUST 7, 1942, exactly eight months after Pearl Harbor, American Marines landed on Guadalcanal in the southern Solomon Islands, as the first step on the long road to Tokyo. The Japanese reacted violently. They elected to have it out right there—to stop the Allied recovery right at the start and at all costs.

Down from their mighty base at Rabaul, they sent reinforcements and supplies through a sea lane flanked by two parallel rows of islands in the Solomons archipelago. The sea lane quickly became known as The Slot, and the supply ships, usually fast destroyers, became known as the Tokyo Express.

The night runs of the Tokyo Express were wearing down the Marines. As they became more and more dirty and tired they became more and more irritated to find that the Japanese they killed were dressed in spruce new uniforms—sure sign that they were newcomers to the island.

Even worse was the sleep-robbing uproar of the

night naval bombardments that pounded planes and installations at Henderson Field on Guadalcanal, the only American base where friendly fighters and bombers could find a home. The American hold on the island was in danger from sheer physical fatigue.

The American and Japanese fleets clashed in the waters around the Guadalcanal landing beaches in a series of bloody surface battles that devoured ships and men on both sides in a hideous contest of attrition. Whichever side could hang on fifteen seconds longer than the other — whichever side could stand to lose one more ship and one more sailor — was going to win.

At the very moment of one of the big cruiser-destroyer clashes (October 11-12, 1942) — officially called the Battle of Cape Esperance — American naval reinforcements of a sort arrived in the area. Forty miles east of the battle, four fresh, unbloodied fighting ships were sailing into Tulagi Harbor at Florida Island, just across a narrow strait from Guadalcanal.

It was half of Motor Torpedo Boat Squadron Three, four PT boats, the first American torpedo boats to arrive in combat waters since the last boat of Lieut. John Bulkeley's disbanded Squadron Three had been burned in the Philippines seven months before.

The PT sailors came topside as they entered the

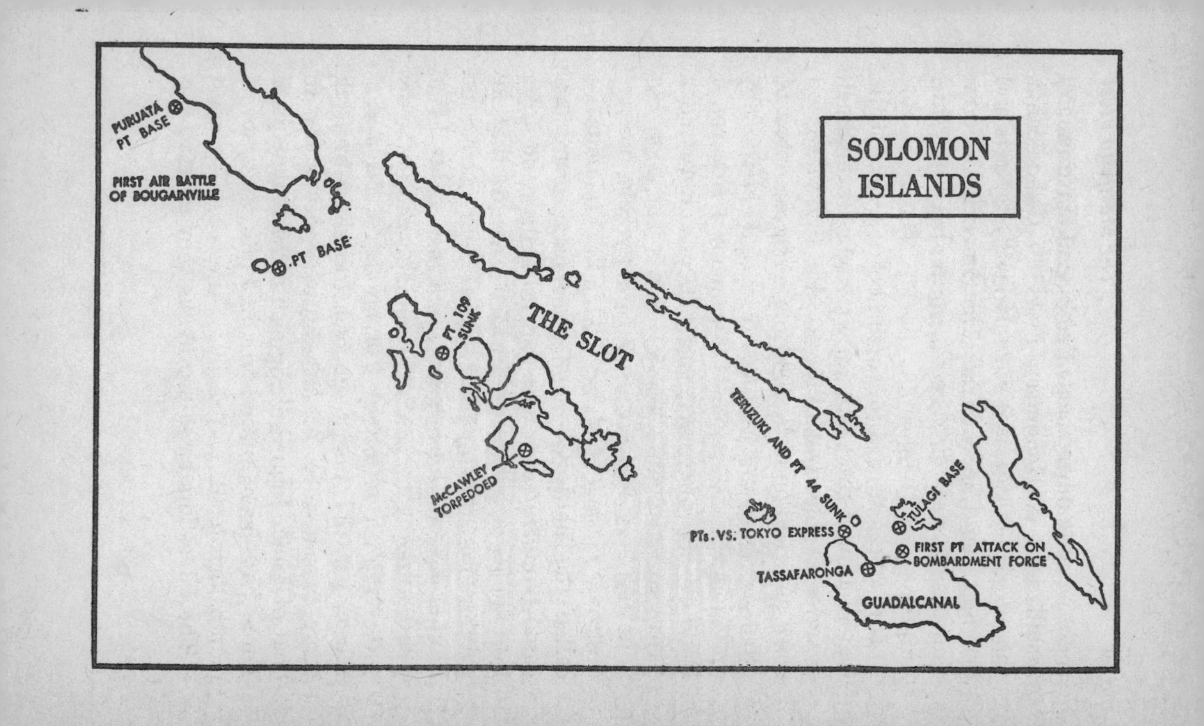
SOLOMON ISLANDS
PURUATÁ PT BASE
FIRST AIR BATTLE OF BOUGAINVILLE
PT BASE
THE SLOT
PT 109 SUNK
McCAWLEY TORPEDOED
TERUZUKI AND PT 44 SUNK
TULAGI BASE
PTs. VS. TOKYO EXPRESS
FIRST PT ATTACK ON BOMBARDMENT FORCE
TASSAFARONGA
GUADALCANAL

harbor to watch the flash of cannonading in the sky to the west where American and Japanese sailors were blowing each other to bloody bits. For them, training time was over, the shooting time was now, and the PT navy was once again on the firing line.

All day on October 13, the PT sailors scurried about, getting the little warships ready for a fight. Their preparations made only a ripple in the maelstrom of activity around the islands.

Coast watchers—friendly observers who hid on islands behind the Japanese lines and reported by radio on ship and plane movements—reported a new menace to Guadalcanal. They had spotted a Japanese naval force coming down The Slot, but they said it was made up only of destroyers.

When Lieut. Commander Alan R. Montgomery, the PT squadron commander at Tulagi, heard that only destroyers were coming, he begged off from the fight—on the extraordinary grounds that he preferred waiting for bigger game.

Montgomery's decision is not as cocky as it first sounds. The Japanese presumably did not know about the arrival of the PTs on the scene, and if ever a PT was going to shoot a torpedo into a big one—a cruiser or a battleship—it was going to be by surprise. No use tipping off the enemy until the big chance came.

The big chance was really on the way. The coast watchers had underestimated the size of the Japanese force. It was actually built around a pair of battleships, escorted by cruisers and destroyers, all bent on pounding Henderson Field and its pesky planes out of existence.

The Japanese command obviously expected no American naval resistance, because ammunition hoists of the Japanese fleet were loaded with a new kind of thin-skinned shell especially designed for blowing into jagged fragments that would slice planes and people to useless shreds. The bombardment shells would not be much use against armor. The Japanese ammunition load would have been a disaster for the task force if it had run into armored opposition — cruisers or battleships of the American Navy — but the Japanese knew as well as we did that there was little likelihood our badly mauled fleet, manned by exhausted sailors, would be anywhere near the scene. The Japanese sailed down The Slot with one hand voluntarily tied behind them, in a sense, supremely confident that they could pound Henderson Field without interference.

Shortly after midnight on October 14th, two Japanese battleships opened up on Henderson Field with gigantic 14-inch rifles shooting the special fragmentation and incendiary shells. The two battleships were accompanied by a cruiser and either eight or nine destroyers. A Japanese scouting plane dropped flares to make the shooting easier.

An American searchlight at Lunga Point, on Guadalcanal, probed over the water, looking for the Japanese, but American 5-inch guns — the largest American guns ashore — were too short of range to reach the battleships and cruisers even if the searchlight had found them. The big ships hove to and poured in a merciless cascade of explosive.

For almost an hour and a half, Marines, soldiers and Seabees lay in foxholes and suffered while the Cyclopean 14-inchers tore holes in the field, riddled planes with shell fragments, started fires and filled the air with shards from exploding shell casings — shards that could slice a man in two without even changing the pitch of his screams.

At the PT base in Tulagi, Lieut. Commander Montgomery was awakened by the din across the way. He knew that no destroyer force could make that kind of uproar. The earth-shaking cannonading meant that the big boys were shooting up Guadalcanal, blithly assuming that the U. S. Navy was not present.

But it was. Motor Torpedo Boat Squadron Three was on the scene and waiting for just such a target.

Montgomery called in his four young skippers—Lieuts. (jg) Henry S. (Stilly) Taylor of PT 46, Robert C. Wark of PT 48, John M. Searles of PT 60, and his brother Robert Searles of PT 38.

At two o'clock in the morning of October 14th, Commander Montgomery ordered: "Prepare for action. All boats under way immediately."

It was the first combat order given to PT boats since the debacle in the Philippines.

The PTs left the harbor together but scattered quickly. They had all spotted the Japanese bombardment fleet by the orange flashes of its guns, and they lost each other in the darkness as they deployed to attack.

Somebody on a Japanese cruiser must have been at least mildly nervous, for a searchlight came on, swept the water toward Tulagi, zipped right across Bob Searles in 38, and then went black. Searles stretched his luck; he cut his speed to 10 knots and began a slow stalk of the cruiser that had muffed its chance to sound the alarm.

So cocky were the Japanese that the cruiser was almost dead in the water; even at 10 knots, the 38 closed the range from behind.

Bob Searles greased the 38 along the still waters of the sound, holding his breath and dreading to see the glare of that searchlight again. He could see the target clearly silhouetted in the gun flashes, and it was a brute – a light cruiser, Bob thought, judging from its shape, its size, and the roar of its guns. Searles figured that he would probably be the first and only PT skipper to enjoy the carefully preserved surprise that the PT sailors hoped would bag them a big one – so he had to make his first shot good or waste the chance they had all been hoarding.

A torpedo, like any other weapon that has to be

aimed, is more likely to hit the closer you get to your target before you shoot. So Bob went in to 400 yards in stealthy silence. Four hundred yards in a naval battle is the equivalent of arm's length in an infantry fire fight. At 400 yards, a spread of torpedoes will usually score, but the machine guns and autocannon of a cruiser's secondary battery, guided by a searchlight, will almost certainly tear up a torpedo boat. Searles, just to be sure of a hit, was doing the same thing as a commando would do if, armed with a high-powered rifle, he crept to within five feet of a sentry armed with a sawed-off shotgun. At any range that rifle is a deadly weapon – like a torpedo – but at close range the shotgun is just as deadly and ten times surer of hitting with the first shot.

At 400 yards Bob fired two fish. He chased along behind them to 200-yard range – almost rock-throwing range – and fired his last two torpedoes. The instant he felt the boat jump from those shots, he poured on the coal and roared past the cruiser, 100 yards astern. As they went by, all hands topside on the PT felt the scorching blast of a double explosion forward of the cruiser's bridge.

The surprise was over. From here on the whole Japanese task force would be alarmed and shooting back – but that big boy the PT sailors had been after was in the bag. The 38's crew was sure of it. Searles had the good sense not to hang around the hornet's nest he had stirred up. His torpedoes were gone anyhow, so he lit out for home, convinced that he had scored the first PT victory of the comeback trail.

The other PTs had scattered, looking for other targets in the dark. There were plenty of targets, for they had penetrated the destroyer screen, without either side knowing it, and were in the heart of the Japanese formation. After the blast from the 38's torpedo attack on the cruiser, the PTs themselves were as much targets as they were hunters.

Lieut. Commander Montgomery, riding with John Searles on the 60, was stalking a big ship – possibly the same cruiser Bob Searles had already attacked – but the escorting destroyers were roiled up and rallying around.

A searchlight poked about the water, looking for the 60 which had probably been dimly spotted by a lookout. The searchlight never found the 60, but it did silhouette the PT for another destroyer. Japanese shells from the second destroyer screamed over the PT, but Montgomery held steadily to his attack course on the cruiser – or whatever it was – until two of the 60's fish were off and running

John Searles spun the rudder over hard left and shoved the throttles up to the stops. Smoke poured from the generator on the stern, to cover their escape, and so the crew of the 60 didn't see the end of the torpedo run, but it claimed a hit, anyhow, from the sound of a massive explosion.

If it was a torpedo hit and if the hit was on the same cruiser Bob Searles said he hit, that cruiser was in sad shape. Not so the destroyers. They were full of fight and boring in on the 60.

Smoke makes a fine screen for covering escape, but only for a time. After the initial escape is successful, a continuing smoke cloud only marks the course of the fleeing PT boat, just as a tracer's phosphorescent trail tracks a bullet through the night. So Montgomery shut off the smoke when he thought they were free, but he had waited a moment too long.

Just as the smoke-screen generator hissed to a halt, a destroyer pinned the 60 down in the blue glare of a searchlight and a salvo of Japanese shells, landing 20 feet astern, almost lifted the 60 out of the water.

The Japanese destroyer captain did not know it, probably still doesn't know it if he is even alive, but when he turned his light on the 60, he simultaneously lost the chance to sink one PT boat by ramming and just possibly saved his own ship from being sunk by still another PT.

Robert Wark's 48 was sneaking up on the destroyer in a torpedo attack on one side; Henry Taylor's 46 was roaring across the water, looking for targets on the other side, quite unaware that the destroyer was in its path. When the searchlight glare hit the 60, Taylor saw the Japanese ship dead ahead and put the rudder of the 46 over hard. He barely missed a collision with the can, a collision that would have reduced his little warship to a floating carpet of matchsticks. But, in skimming by the destroyer, Taylor almost rammed Wark's 48 and spoiled its torpedo attack. Wark lost contact with the destroyer in the wild careering around the sound that followed the double near-collision, and he didn't get off his torpedoes.

The whole time the Japanese captain was so intent on sinking the 60, pinned down by his searchlight, he apparently missed the near-collisions right under his nose. His shells were creeping up the wake of the fleeting 60 and he doggedly plowed into the stream of 50-caliber bullets from the PT antiaircraft machine-gun battery, willing to take the punishment in exchange for a chance to run the torpedo boat down.

Lieut. Commander Montgomery turned on the smoke generator again and had the inspiration to drop two depth charges into his wake. The charges exploded just ahead of the Japanese destroyer, and the Japanese skipper shied away from the chase, fearful that the closer he got to the PT boat, the more likely he was to be blown in two by a depth charge right under the bridge. The 60 escaped in the smoke, lay close to the beach for the rest of that night, and drifted aground on a coral reef near morning.

Wark, who had picked up his original target again, was still trying to shoot a fish into the destroyer that had abandoned the chase of the 60. Wark did not know it, but he was himself being stalked. From 200 yards away, a Japanese destroyer caught the 48 in a searchlight beam and fired all the guns that would bear.

A searchlight beam is a two-edged tool. It helps the aim of the gunners on the destroyer; at the same time it makes a beautiful mark for the PT's machine guns. C. E. Todd, the ship's cook, pumped 50-caliber bullets into the destroyer's bridge and superstructure until the light was shattered. The destroyer disappeared and nobody knows what damage it suffered, but it is highly improbable that it could be raked by 50-caliber fire from 200 yards away without serious damage and casualties.

The 48's skipper could say: "He never laid a glove on me."

Aboard the Japanese flagship, the admiral, apparently alarmed by unexpected naval resistance no matter how puny, ordered a cease fire and a withdrawal. Eighty minutes of shellfire had left Henderson Field in a shambles anyhow. Forever after, Guadalcanal veterans of the night between

October 13 and 14, 1942, talked about The Bombardment—not the bombardment of this date or the bombardment of that date. Simply The Bombardment. Everybody knew which one they meant.

What had the PTs accomplished on their first sortie? Bob and John Searles claimed solid hits on a cruiser. Postwar assessment of claims says that there is "no conclusive evidence that any major Japanese ship was sunk" on that night. But the next day a coast watcher reported that natives had seen a large warship sink off the New Georgia coast, to the north on the withdrawal route. Radio Tokyo itself acknowledged the loss of a cruiser that night under the attack of "nineteen torpedo boats of which we destroyed fourteen."

That last bit—public admission by the Japanese of the loss of a cruiser to a PT—is the most convincing. The Japanese played down their own losses ridiculously. Sometimes they even believed their own propaganda, so much so that they deployed for battle forces which had been destroyed but whose loss they had never admitted, even to themselves.

A curious incident during the almost nightly naval bombardments of Henderson Field shows the Japanese sailor's fatal desire to believe his own propaganda. Eight Japanese destroyers and a light cruiser bombarded the field the night of October 25, 1942. They sank two small ships, but they called off the shore bombardment after only a feeble effort.

The reason?

A Japanese officer ashore had sent a message: BANZAI. OCCUPIED AIRFIELD AT 2300.

He had done no such thing. Indeed, the very planes spared by that spurious message sank the cruiser the next morning.

Perhaps a more important result of the first PT foray than the hit on a cruiser was the shock to the Japanese nervous system. The Japanese navy had an inordinate horror of torpedo boats — possibly because the Japanese themselves were so diabolically good at surface torpedo attack. The knowledge that American torpedo boats were back on the scene must have been a jolt to their sensitivities.

Nobody can prove that the Japanese admiral called off the bombardment because of the torpedo attacks — after all, he had already shot up Henderson Field for eighty minutes and had expended almost all his special bombardment ammunition — but it is a remarkable coincidence that the shooting stopped almost immediately after the PTs arrived, and the withdrawal followed soon after the torpedoes started swimming around.

Half an hour after their sortie from Tulagi, the PTs saw a vast armada of Japanese ships turn tail and leave the field to them.

The Marines didn't quibble. They crawled out of their foxholes, those who could, and thanked God for whoever had run off the 14-inchers. Henderson Field had survived, but barely, and the Marines were willing to give anybody credit for running off the battleships, if whoever it was would just keep them off. The PTs were willing to try.

The night between October 14th and 15th was the low point of the Navy's contribution to the Guadalcanal campaign. Two Japanese cruisers insolently pounded Henderson Field with 752 eight-inch shells, and the Navy could not lift a finger to stop them. The only Navy fighting ships in the area were the four PTs of Squadron Three, but the 60 was still aground on a reef, the 38 had left all of its torpedoes inside a Japanese cruiser the night before, and the other two PTs were escorting two little supply ships across the channel between Tulagi and Guadalcanal. The cruisers had a field day.

The next night two Japanese cruisers fired 1,500 punishing eight-inch shells at Henderson Field.

Secretary of the Navy Frank Knox, in Washington, after studying the battle report, could say only: "Everybody *hopes* we can hang on."

Admiral Chester Nimitz was even more grim. "It now appears that we are unable to control the sea in the Guadalcanal area. Thus our supply of the positions will only be done at great expense to us. The situation is not hopeless, but it is certainly critical."

Perhaps the PTs had arrived too late to do any good. Certainly a navy that consisted of three torpedo boats afloat and one on a reef was not going to win the battle for Guadalcanal.

The Japanese, beginning on November 2nd, spent a week running destroyer and cruiser deckloads of soldiers down The Slot—65 destroyer deckloads and two cruiser loads in all.

On November 8th, PTs hit the destroyer *Mochizuki* but did not sink it.

This kind of reinforcement by dribbles was not fast enough to satisfy the Japanese brass, so they planned to stop sending a boy to do a man's job. At Truk, they organized a mighty task force of two light carriers, four battleships, 11 cruisers and 36 destroyers to escort 11 fast transports to Guadalcanal on November 14th.

Before risking the transports, jammed with soldiers to be landed at Tassafaronga, the Japanese planned to bombard Henderson Field for two straight nights to eliminate once and for all the dangerous Marine airplanes based there.

The climactic sea struggle for Guadalcanal began on the night of November 12, 1942.

American scouting planes and Allied coast watchers sent word that a frighteningly powerful bombardment force was on its way down The Slot, and the most optimistic defenders of Guadalcanal wondered if this was going to be the end.

Two Japanese battleships, the *Hiei* and the *Kirishima,* a cruiser, and fourteen destroyers were in the Japanese fleet. (The Japanese had learned to fear the PT boats of Tulagi; the fleet commander had posted two destroyers on one advanced flank and three destroyers on the other, as a torpedo-boat screen. In addition, he had assigned three other destroyers, not counted among the 14 under his direct command, to rove ahead on an anti-PT patrol.)

In a swirling, half-hour action on Friday, November 13th – the opening of the three-day naval Battle of Guadalcanal – the United States Navy lost the cruiser *Atlanta,* the destroyers *Barton, Cushing, Laffey,* and *Monssen,* and suffered severe damage to the cruisers *Portland, San Francisco, Helena, Juneau,* and to three destroyers. Admiral Daniel J. Callaghan was killed.

Limping home after the battle, the cruiser *Juneau* was torpedoed by the submarine I-26 (whose skipper admits that he was aiming at another ship entirely). The *Juneau* disappeared in a blast of smoke and flame. In one of the most tragic and inexplicable misadventures of the war, the survivors of the *Juneau,* floating within easy reach of the PTs at Tulagi, were abandoned, and no attempt was made to rescue them until all but a handful had died of exposure.

It is possible that the PTs – excellent rescue

craft manned by sailors eager to help stricken shipmates—were so new to the theatre that the top brass didn't even know of their presence, or at least weren't in the habit of thinking about them. At any rate, the PTs were tied up at Tulagi while Amercan sailors drowned almost within sight of the harbor.

On the night between November 13th and 14th, two Japanese heavy cruisers, screened by a light cruiser and four destroyers, steamed toward Guadalcanal with another load of bombardment shells.

The situation on Guadalcanal was grave. The base was crammed with the sick and weary survivors of the naval battle. The veteran defenders knew another punishing flotilla was on its way with possibly the final, fatal load of fragmentation shells aboard—and there were no big American ships near enough to say them nay.

The United States Navy had almost shot its bolt, at least temporarily. Almost but not quite.

Two PTs were still in the fight.

One, commanded by Stilly Taylor, and another, commanded by John Searles, had been screening the heavy cruiser *Portland,* which had been badly damaged in the previous night's battle and was being towed to Tulagi.

Stilly Taylor tells what happened in one of the most momentously important torpedo-boat adventures of the Pacific War:

"The Japs began to shell Henderson Field, first

putting a very bright flare in the vicinity of the field, and so naturally both of us [the two PTs] started in on them independently. . . .

"As soon as the Japs opened fire it was obvious to us that there was at least one fairly heavy ship. We thought it was probably a battleship. . . . We could tell it was definitely a heavy ship because of the long orange flash from its gunfire rather than the short white flash which we knew from experience was the smaller fire of the destroyers. . . .

"Due to the light put up by the Nip flares, I was able to use my director for the first time. I set the target's speed at about 20 knots, and I think he was doing slightly more than this. I kept him in the director for approximately seven of his salvos and really had a beautiful line on him. [PT boats usually were forced, by bad visibility at night and in bad weather, to shoot from the hip. A chance to use a director for visually aimed fire was an unaccustomed luxury well worth gloating over in an action report.]

"After closing to about 1,000 yards, I decided that if we went in any farther we would get tangled up in the destroyer screen which I knew would be surrounding him at about 500 to 700 yards.

"I therefore fired three fish. The fourth misfired and never left the tube. The three fish landed beautifully and made no flash as we fired them.

"We immediately turned around and started back

for the base, but we had the torpedoes running hot and straight toward the target.

"I am positive that at least one of them found its mark.

"Certainly the Nips ceased fire immediately and apparently turned right around and limped home."

Nobody knows what damage these two PTs did that night. Planes the next day found a badly damaged cruiser leaving the scene, and that could well have been Taylor's victim. At any rate, the material damage inflicted by these two brave seamen and their crews is comparatively unimportant.

What is important is the almost incredible but quite possible fact that the two cockleshells ran off a horribly dangerous Japanese surface fleet prepared to give Henderson Field what might well have been its death blow. As soon as the torpedo boats attacked, the Japanese stopped shooting and ran.

It is not hard to understand why. The American fleet had been badly battered during the previous night's battle, but so had the Japanese fleet, and Japanese nerves were probably raw and jumpy.

The two PTs achieved complete surprise, and a surprise attack in restricted waters is always unsettling to naval officers, even the most cocksure and well rested. The Japanese could not be sure exactly who was attacking and in what force. They could have had only a dim idea of what damage they had done to the American Navy the night before, and, for all they knew, the torpedo tracks they saw came from a dangerous destroyer flotilla, backed up by who knows how many mighty ships of the line.

With their nerves shaken by the suddenness of the torpedo attack and with no knowledge of what was prowling around out there in the dark, it apparently seemed best to the Japanese commanders to abandon the bombardment quickly and save their ships for another day.

The two glorified cabin cruisers had driven off the Japanese task force when only three planes had been destroyed and 17 damaged (all the damaged planes were in the air before the end of the next day), and Henderson Field was still in action. The next day, November 14th, a smoothly functioning Henderson Field was host not only to the Marine planes permanently based there but also to Navy planes from the carrier *Enterprise* which landed at Henderson for refueling during shuttle trips to attack 11 fast Japanese transports coming down The Slot.

All-day attacks on November 14th, by the Marine, Navy, and Army planes, saved from destruction by the two PT boats, sank seven of the transports and worked a hideous massacre among the Japanese soldiers on their decks and in their holds. Four of the transports and 11 destroyers survived and at sunset were sailing for the Japanese beachhead of Tassafaronga Point. The destroyers carried deckloads of survivors from the sunken transports.

The destroyer commander was Rear Admiral Raizo Tanaka, perhaps the most brilliant combat officer of the Japanese navy. He repeatedly showed a fantastic devotion to duty that enabled him to carry out his missions in spite of seemingly impossible difficulties. Tanaka *was* the Tokyo Express.

To give Tanaka a little help with the disembarkation of the troops at Guadalcanal, the Japanese planned to bombard Henderson during the landings as a diversion—and just possibly as a *coup de grâce* to further American air resistance. They sent a battleship, two heavy cruisers, two light cruisers and nine destroyers to do the job. This time the light cruisers and destroyers were deployed in a formidable anti-torpedo-boat screen to prevent a recurrence of the previous night's spooking from a measly two-boat PT raid.

The Japanese had lost their chance, however, for much more American naval power than a brace of torpedo boats stood between the Japanese and Henderson Field. Admiral W. A. Lee, on the battleship *Washington*, had arrived from the south, accompanied by the battleship *South Dakota* and four destroyers. He sailed north to meet the Japanese across Iron Bottom Bay (so called because the bottom was littered with the hulks of Japanese and American ships sunk in earlier battles. There were so many hulls on the ocean's floor that quartermasters reported to their skippers that magnetic compasses were deflected by the scrap iron).

The American admiral – known to his intimates as "Ching" Lee – had a bad moment when he overheard two PTs gossiping about his battleships over the voice radio.

"There go two big ones, but I don't know whose they are," said one PT skipper.

Admiral Lee grabbed the microphone and quickly identified himself to shore headquarters before the PTs could get off a nervous shot.

"Refer your big boss about Ching Lee; Chinese, catchee? Call off your boys."

The PT skippers answered, with good humor, that they were well acquainted with old "Ching" and promised not to go after him.

The PT crews watched Admiral Lee sail into the decisive last action of the three-day Battle of Guadalcanal. That night his ships sank the Japanese battleship and routed the Japanese bombardment fleet. But the mixed transport and destroyer reinforcement flotilla was taken, nevertheless, by the stubborn and wily Admiral Tanaka, around the action and to the beach at Tassafaronga where he carried out his reinforcement mission almost literally "come hell or high water."

The Japanese had made a mighty effort, but American fliers, sailors, and PT boatmen had spoiled the assault. The only profit to the Japanese from the bloody three days was the landing of

2,000 badly shaken soldiers, 260 cases of ammunition, and 1,500 bags of rice.

But the Japanese were not totally discouraged. They had the redoubtable Tanaka on their side, and so they went back to supply by the Tokyo Express. The idea was for Tanaka's fast destroyers to run down The Slot by night to Tassafaronga Point, where sailors would push overboard drums of supplies. Troops ashore would then round up the floating drums in small boats. In that way, Tanaka's fast destroyers would not have to stop moving and would make a less tempting target for the Tulagi PTs than a transport at anchor.

On November 30, 1942, Admiral Tanaka shoved off from Bougainville Island with eight destroyers loaded with 1,100 drums of supplies. At the same moment an American task force of five cruisers and six destroyers — a most formidable task force indeed, especially for a night action — left the American base at Espiritu Santo to break up just the kind of supply run Tanaka was undertaking.

The two forces converged on Tassafaronga Point from opposite directions. The American force enormously outgunned Tanaka's destroyers and also had the tremendous advantage of being, to some extent, equipped with radar, then a brand-new and little-understood gadget. Thus the American force could expect to enjoy an additional superiority of surprise.

And that is just the way it worked out. At 11:06 P.M., American radar picked up Tanaka's ships. Admiral Tanaka's comparatively feeble flotilla was blindly sailing into a trap.

American destroyers fired twenty torpedoes at the still unsuspecting Japanese, who did not wake up to their danger until the cruisers opened fire with main battery guns at five-mile range.

The Japanese lashed back with a reflex almost as automatic for Tanaka's well-drilled destroyer sailors as jerking a finger back from a red-hot stove. They instantly filled the water with torpedoes.

No American torpedoes scored. Six Japanese torpedoes hit four American cruisers, sinking *Northampton,* and damaging *Pensacola, Minneapolis,* and *New Orleans* so seriously that they were unfit for action for almost a year. Cruiser gunfire sank one Japanese destroyer, but the rest of Admiral Tanaka's ships, besides giving the vastly superior American force a stunning defeat, even managed to push overboard many of the drums they had been sent down to deliver.

Tanaka had once more carried out his mission and had won a great naval victory, almost as a sideline to the main business.

On the first anniversary of Pearl Harbor, December 7, 1942, Admiral Tanaka came down again with eleven destroyers.

This time it was not a mighty cruiser-destroyer

force waiting for him, but only eight PTs from Tulagi. They were manned, however, by some of the most aggressive officers and men in the American Navy. The boats were deployed around Cape Esperance and Savo Island, on the approaches to Tassafaronga.

Two patrolling torpedo boats spotted Tanaka's destroyers and attacked, but one broke down and the other came to his rescue, so no shots were fired. Nevertheless, the Admiral was spooked by the abortive attack of two diminutive PTs, and retreated. He recovered his courage in a few minutes and tried again.

This time four PTs jumped him and fired twelve torpedoes. When their tubes were empty, the PTs roared by the destroyers, strafing with their machine guns—and being strafed. Jack Searles, in 59, passed down the *Oyashio*'s side less than a hundred yards away, raking the destroyer's superstructure and gun crews with 50-caliber fire. The 59 itself was also riddled, of course, but stayed afloat.

Admiral Tanaka, who had run around the blazing duel of battlewagons at the Battle of Guadalcanal to deliver his reinforcements, who had bored through massive day-long air attacks, who had gutted a mighty cruiser force to deliver his cargo to Tassafaronga, turned back before the threat of four PTs, abandoned the mission, and fled back to Bougainville.

The PT navy at Tulagi (and the Marines and soldiers on Guadalcanal) had good cause to celebrate a clear-cut victory on this first anniversary of Pearl Harbor.

Times were too hard for the PTs to get any rest. Jack Searles patched up his bullet-torn 59, and, with another boat, put out two nights later, on December 9th, to machine-gun a Japanese landing barge sighted near Cape Esperance. During the barge-PT duel, one of Searles' lookouts spotted a submarine on the surface, oozing along at about two knots. Jack whipped off two quick shots and blew a 2,000-ton blockade-running submarine (I-3) into very small pieces. There is no way to deny the submarine to Jack Searles' bag, because a Japanese naval officer, the sole survivor, swam ashore and told the story of the I-3's last moments.

On the night of December 11th Admiral Tanaka began another run of the Tokyo Express with ten destroyers. Dive bombers attacked during daylight, but made no hits. The job of stopping Tanaka's Tokyo Express was passed to the PTs. They zipped out of the harbor at Tulagi and deployed along the beach between Tassafaronga and Cape Esperance.

The night was bright and clear, and shortly after midnight three PTs, commanded by Lieut. (jg) Lester H. Gamble, saw the destroyer column and attacked. The other two boats were skippered by Stilly Taylor and Lieut. (jg) William E. Kreiner III.

The Japanese destroyers turned on searchlights and let go with main batteries and machine guns, but the three torpedo boats got off their torpedoes and popped two solid hits into the destroyer *Teruzuki.* The Japanese ship blazed up, and for the second time Tanaka had had enough of torpedo boats. He went home.

The PTs had not yet had enough of Tanaka, however, for Lieut. Frank Freeland's 44 heard the combat talk of his squadron mates on the voice radio, and came running. He roared past the burning *Teruzuki,* chasing the retreating destroyers. Two things were working against him; Lieut. Freeland did not know it, but one of the destroyers had stayed behind with the *Teruzuki,* and the flames from the burning ship were lighting the PT boat beautifully for the hidden Japanese gunners.

Aboard the 44 was Lieut. (jg) Charles M. Melhorn, who reports his version of what happened:

"We were throwing up quite a wake, and with the burning cargo ship [he probably mistook the burning *Teruzuki* for a cargo ship] lighting up the whole area I thought we would soon be easy pickings and I told the skipper so. Before he could reply, Crowe, the quartermaster who was at the wheel, pointed and yelled out 'Destroyer on the starboard bow. There's your target, Captain.'

"Through the glasses I could make out a destroyer two points on our starboard bow, distant about 8,000 yards, course south-southwest. We came right and started our run. We had no sooner steadied on our new course than I picked up two more destroyers through my glasses. They were in column thirty degrees on our port bow, target course 270, coming up fast.

"The skipper and I both saw at once that continuing our present course would pin us against the beach and lay us wide open to broadsides from at least three Jap cans. The Skipper shifted targets to the two destroyers, still about 4,000 yards off, and we started in again.

"By this time we were directly between the blazing ship and the two destroyers. As we started the run I kept looking for the can that had fired. . . . I picked him up behind and to the left of our targets. He was swinging, apparently to form up in column astern of the other two. The trap was sprung, and as I pointed out this fourth destroyer the lead ship in the column opened fire."

The 44 escaped from the destroyer ambush behind a smoke screen, but once clear, turned about for a second attack. The burning *Teruzuki* illuminated the 44, and *Teruzuki's* guardian destroyer, lurking in the dark, drew a bead on the ambushed PT.

"We had just come out of our turn when we were fired on. . . . I saw the blast, yelled 'That's for us,' and jumped down on the portside by the cockpit. We were hit aft in the engine room.

"I don't remember much. For a few seconds nothing registered at all. I looked back and saw a gaping hole in what was once the engine-room canopy. The perimeter of the hole was ringed by little tongues of flame. I looked down into the water and saw we had lost way.

"Someone on the bow said 'Shall we abandon ship?' Freeland gave the order to go ahead and abandon ship.

"I stayed at the cockpit . . . glancing over where the shell came from. He let go again.

"I dove . . . I dove deep and was still under when the salvo struck. The concussion jarred me badly, but I kept swimming underwater. There was a tremendous explosion, paralyzing me from the waist down. The water around me went red.

"The life jacket took control and pulled me to the surface. I came up in a sea of fire, the flaming embers of the boat cascading all about me. I tried to get free of the life jacket but couldn't. I started swimming feebly. I thought the game was up, but the water which had shot sky high in the explosion rained down and put out the fires around me. . . .

"I took a few strokes away from the gasoline fire, which was raging about fifteen yards behind me, and as I turned back I saw two heads, one still helmeted, between me and the flames. I called to the two men and told them that I expected the Japs to be over in short order to machine-gun us, and to get their life jackets ready to slip. I told them to get clear of the reflection of the fire as quickly as possible, and proceeded to do so myself.

"I struck out for Savo, whose skyline ridge I could see dimly, and gradually made headway toward shore. Every two or three minutes I stopped to look back for other survivors or an approaching destroyer, but saw nothing save the boat which was burning steadily, and beyond it the [*Teruzuki*] which burned and exploded all night long.

"Sometime shortly before dawn a PT boat cruised up and down off Savo and passed about twenty-five yards ahead of me. I was all set to hail him when I looked over my shoulder and saw a Jap can bearing down on his starboard quarter.

"I didn't know whether the PT was maneuvering to get a shot at him or not, so I kept my mouth shut. I let him go by, slipped my life jacket, and waited for the fireworks.

"The Jap can lay motionless for some minutes, and I finally made it out as nothing more than a destroyer-shaped shadow formed by the fires and smoke.

"I judge that I finally got ashore on Savo about 0730 or 0800. Lieutenant Stilly Taylor picked me up off the beach about an hour later."

Lieut. Melhorn was in the water between five and six hours. Only one other sailor survived the explosion of the 44's gas tank. Two officers and seven enlisted men died.

Flames on the *Teruzuki* — the same flames that lit the way to its fiery death for the 44 — finally ate their way into the depth-charge magazine, and just before dawn the Japanese destroyer went up with a jarring crash.

More important to the fighters on Guadalcanal than the sinking of the *Teruzuki* was the astonishing and gratifying fact that Admiral Tanaka, the destroyer tiger, had been turned back one more time by a handful of wooden cockleshells, without landing his supplies. The big brass of the cruiser fleet that had been unable to stop Tanaka at the Battle of Tassafaronga must have been bewildered.

After the clash between Tanaka and the torpedo boats on December 11th, no runs of the Tokyo Express were attempted for three weeks. The long lull meant dull duty for the PTs, but was a proof of their effectiveness in derailing the Tokyo Express. Japanese soldiers on Guadalcanal were down to eating roots and leaves — and sometimes even other Japanese, according to persistent reports among the Japanese themselves — before their navy worked up enough nerve to try another run of the Tokyo Express.

On January 2nd, ten destroyers came down The Slot. One was damaged by a dive bomber's near miss, and another was detached to escort the cripple, but the other eight sailed on.

That night, eleven PTs attacked Tanaka's destroyers with eighteen torpedoes, but had no luck. Tanaka unloaded his drums and was gone before dawn.

No matter. As soon as the sun came up, the PTs puttered about Iron Bottom Bay, enjoying a bit of target practice on the drums pushed off the destroyers' decks. One way or the other, the torpedo boats of Tulagi snatched food from the mouths of the starving Japanese garrison.

A week later a coast watcher up the line called in word that Tanaka was running eight destroyers down The Slot. Rouse out the PTs again!

Just after midnight on January 13th, Lieut. Rollin Westholm, in PT 112, saw four destroyers and called for a coordinated attack with Lieut. (jg) Charles E. Tilden's 43.

"Make 'em good," Lieut. Westholm said, so Lieut. Tilden took his 43 into 400-yard range before firing two. Both missed. To add to his disastrous bad luck, the port tube flashed a bright red light, a blazing giveaway of the 43's position.

The destroyer hit the 43 with the second salvo, and all hands went over the side, diving deep to escape machine-gun strafing. The destroyer passed close enough so that the swimming sailors could hear the Japanese chattering on the deck.

Lieut. Clark W. Faulkner, in 40, drew a bead on the second destroyer in column and fired four. His heart was made glad by what he thought was a juicy hit, so he took his empty tubes back home.

Lieut. Westholm, in 112, took on the third destroyer and was equally certain he had put one into his target, but two of the destroyers had zeroed in during his approach run, and two shells blew his boat open at the waterline. Lieut. Westholm and his eleven shipmates watched the rest of the battle from a life raft. The other PTs fired twelve fish, but didn't even claim any hits.

Either Lieut. Westholm or Lieut. Faulkner had scored, however, for the *Hatsukaze* had caught a torpedo under the wardroom. The Japanese skipper at first despaired of saving his ship, but damage-control parties plugged the hole well enough so that he was able to escape before daylight.

When the sun rose, the PTs still afloat picked up survivors of the two lost torpedo boats and then went through the morning routine of sinking the 250 floating drums of supplies the destroyers had jettisoned. The starving Japanese watching from the beach must have wished all torpedo boats in hell that morning.

The Japanese did come out to tow in the wreckage of the PT 43, but a New Zealand warship stepped in with a few well-placed broadsides and reduced the already splintered torpedo boat to a mess of matchwood before the Japanese could study it.

Nobody but the Japanese High Command knew it at this point, but the plane and PT blockade of the Tokyo Express had won; the island garrison had been starved out.

During the night between February 1st and 2nd, coast watchers reported 20 Japanese destroyers coming down The Slot. The American Navy had no way of knowing it, but the Tokyo Express was running in reverse. The decks of those destroyers were clear—they were being kept clear to make room for a deckload of the starved-out Japanese on Guadalcanal. Japan was finally calling it quits and pulling out of the island.

Whatever the mission of the Japanese ships, the mission of the American Navy was clear—to keep the Japanese from doing whatever it was they were doing and to sink some ships in the process.

Three American mine-layers sprinkled 300 mines north of Guadalcanal, near Savo Island, in the waters where the destroyers might be expected to pass. Eleven PTs waiting in ambush attacked the destroyers as they steamed by the minefield. The PTs rejoiced at a good, solid hit on a destroyer by somebody — nobody was sure whom — and the destroyer *Makigumo* admittedly acquired an enormous hole in the hull at that very moment, but the Japanese skipper said that he hit a mine. He said he never saw any PTs attacking him.

Postwar assessment officers say that he probably hit a mine while maneuvering to avoid a PT torpedo. Avoid a torpedo attack he never even saw? Someone is confused. Some of the PT sailors who were sure of hits on the *Makigumo* have a tendency to get sulky when this minefield business is mentioned, and nobody can blame them. The *Makigumo*, at any rate, had to be scuttled.

Regardless of what damage they did to the Japanese, the PTs themselves suffered terribly in this battle.

Lieut. (jg) J. H. Claggett's 111 was hit by a shell and set afire. The crew swam until morning, fighting off sharks and holding up the wounded. Two torpedo boatmen were killed.

Ensign James J. Kelly's 37 caught a shell on the gas tank and disappeared in a puff of orange flame. One badly wounded man survived.

Ensign Ralph L. Richards' 123 had stalked to within 500 yards of a destroyer target when a Japanese glide bomber slid in from nowhere, dropped a single bomb, and made possibly the most fantastically lucky hit of the war. The bomb landed square on the tiny fantail of the racing PT boat. The boat went up in a blur of flames and splinters. Four men were killed.

In spite of the fierce attacks of the PT flotilla, Tanaka's sailors managed to take the destroyers in to the beach, load a shipment of evacuees, and slip out again for the quick run home.

This was the last and by far the bloodiest action of the PTs in the Guadalcanal campaign. The PTs had lost three boats and seventeen men in the battle and had not scored themselves — unless you count the destroyer *Makigumo*, which PT sailors stubbornly insist is theirs.

An over-all summary of their contribution to the campaign for Guadalcanal, however, gives them a whopping score:

A submarine and a destroyer sunk [not counting *Makigumo*]

Two destroyers badly damaged

Tons of Japanese supply drums riddled and sunk

Dozens of disaster victims pulled from the water

Two massive bombardments just possibly scared off

And — by far the most important credit — the Tokyo Express of Rear Admiral Raizo Tanaka ambushed and definitely turned back twice after a powerful cruiser force had failed at the job.

Even after the postwar assessment teams cut down PT sinking credits to a fraction of PT claims, there is still plenty of credit left for a force ten times the size of the Tulagi fleet.

3.

Battering Down the Gate:

the Western Hinge

TOWARD the end of 1942, as the Japanese defense of Guadalcanal was crumbling, American forces began to inch forward elsewhere in the Pacific, most notably on the island of New Guinea, almost 600 miles to the west of Guadalcanal.

New Guinea is the second largest island in the world (only Greenland is larger). Dropped over the United States, the island would reach from New York City to Houston, Texas; it is big enough to cover all of New England, plus New York, Pennsylvania, Maryland, West Virginia, Ohio, Kentucky, and all of Tennessee, except for Memphis and its suburbs. Even today, vast inland areas are unexplored and possibly some tribes in the mountains have never even heard about the white man — or about the Japanese either, for that matter. The island is shaped like a turkey, with its head and wattles pointed east.

Early in the war, right after the fall of the Philippines and of the East Indies, the Japanese had landed on the turkey's back. The Australians

PHILIPPINE ISLANDS
PT SINKS DESTROYER
KAMIKAZES ATTACK
BATTLE OF SURIGAO STRAITS
MINDANAO
YAP
PALAU IS.
PTs 489 and 363
RESCUE DOWNED PILOT
CELEBES
TIMOR
ARAFURA
SEA

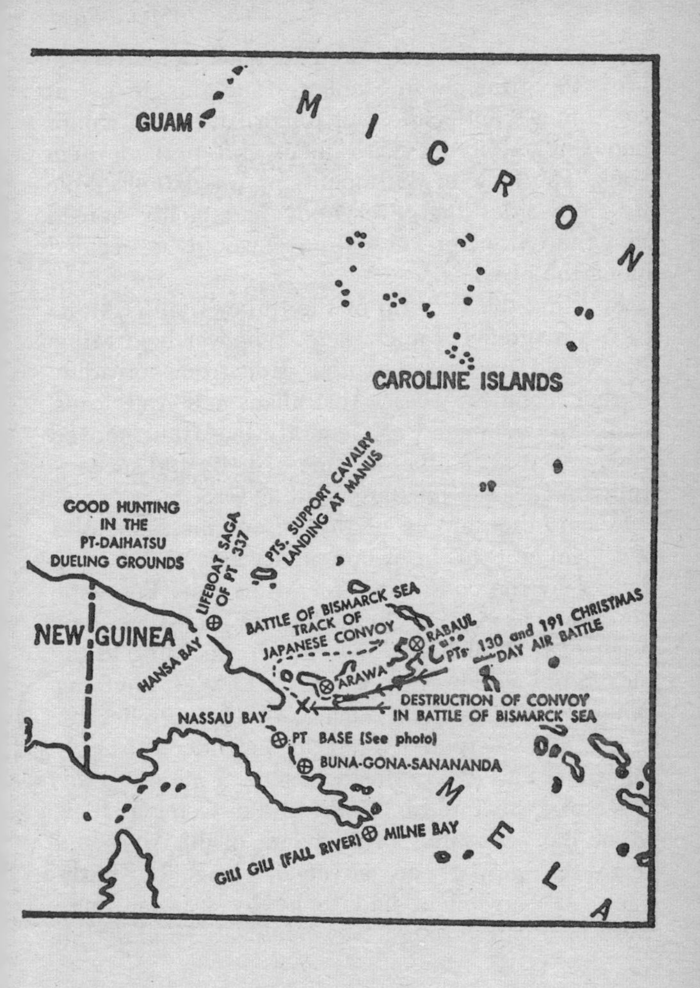
GUAM
MICRON
CAROLINE ISLANDS
PTS. SUPPORT CAVALRY LANDING AT MANUS
GOOD HUNTING IN THE PT-DAIHATSU DUELING GROUNDS
LIFEBOAT SAGA OF PT 337
NEW GUINEA
HANSA BAY
BATTLE OF BISMARCK SEA
TRACK OF JAPANESE CONVOY
RABAUL
PTs 130 and 191 CHRISTMAS DAY AIR BATTLE
ARAWA
DESTRUCTION OF CONVOY IN BATTLE OF BISMARCK SEA
NASSAU BAY
PT BASE (See photo)
BUNA-GONA-SANANANDA
MELA
MILNE BAY
GILI GILI (FALL RIVER)

held the turkey's belly. The Japanese had tried to cross the grim Owen Stanley Mountains, to get at the turkey's underside, but tough Australian troops had slugged it out with them and pushed them back. The fight in the mountains was so miserable for both sides that everybody had tacitly agreed that the battle for New Guinea would be decided along the beaches.

Splitting the very tip of the turkey's tail is Milne Bay, a magnificent anchorage. Whoever held Milne Bay could prevent the other side from spreading farther along the coast. Australians and Americans, under the command of General MacArthur, moved first, seized Milne Bay in June of 1942, and successfully fought off a Japanese landing force.

A curious example of the misery the homefolks can deal out to front-line fighters is the mix-up caused by the code name for Milne Bay. For some obscure reason, the Gili Gili base, at Milne Bay, was called "Fall River." Naturally, according to the inexorable workings of Murphy's Law (if anything *can* go wrong, it *will*) many of the supplies for Milne Bay were delivered to bewildered supply officers at Fall River, Massachusetts.

Despite this foul-up, by the end of October, 1942, Milne Bay was safely in the hands of the Allies and ready to support an advance along the bird's back. All movement had to be by sea, for there were no roads through New Guinea's jungles, and the waters around the turkey's tail were the most poorly charted in the world. Navigators of deep-draft ships were horrified to have to sail through reef- and rock-filled waters, depending on charts with disquieting notes like "Reef possibly seen here by Entrecasteaux in 1791." No naval commander in his right mind would commit deep-draft ships to such uncharted and dangerous waters for nighttime duty. Which means that the times and the coastal waters of eastern New Guinea were made for PT boats, or vice versa.

On December 17, 1942, less than a week after the PTs of Tulagi had fought the last big battle with the *incoming* Tokyo Express, the PT tender *Hilo* towed two torpedo boats into Milne Bay and set up for business. Other PTs followed. For seven more months motor torpedo boats were to be the entire surface striking force of the U. S. Navy in the Solomon Sea around the tail of the New Guinea turkey.

By the time the *Hilo* had arrived at Milne Bay, the fight for the turkey's back had moved 200 miles up the coast to a trio of villages called Buna, Gona, and Sananda. Two hundred miles is too long a haul for PT boats, so the *Hilo* stayed at Milne Bay as a kind of rear base, the main striking force of PTs moving closer to the fighting. They set up camp at Tufi, in the jungles around Oro Bay, almost within sight of the Buna battlefield, and began the nightly coastal patrols that were to stretch on for almost two weary years before all of New Guinea was back in Allied hands.

First blood was drawn on Christmas Eve. Ensign Robert F. Lynch celebrated the holiday by taking out the PT 122 for a routine patrol, looking for small Japanese coasters or submarines running supplies and reinforcements into Buna. The night was dark and rainy, and the PT chugged along without much hope of finding any action. PTs had no radar in those days, and a visual lookout was not very effective in a New Guinea downpour.

Even in New Guinea, however, the rain cannot go on forever. When the rain clouds parted, a bright moon lit up the sea and a lookout snapped to attention.

"Submarine," he hissed. "Dead ahead, a submarine."

Hove to on the surface was a Japanese I-boat, probably waiting for Japanese small craft to come from the beach for supplies, or else recharging its batteries, or probably both. Ensign Lynch began his silent stalk and closed to 1,000 yards without alarming the submarine's crew. He fired two torpedoes and kept on closing the range to 500 yards, where he fired two more. The submarine went up in a geyser of water, scrap iron, and flame.

Ensign Lynch thought he saw a dim shape beyond his victim and was alert when another surfaced I-boat shot four torpedoes at him. He slipped between the torpedo tracks, but could do nothing about retaliating, because he had emptied his tubes. He had to let the second I-boat go. Postwar assessment gives Ensign Lynch a definite kill on this submarine.

The same Christmas Eve, two other PTs from the Oro Bay base sank two barges full of troops.

Ensign Lynch's torpedoing of the submarine – the first combat victory of the PT fleet in New Guinea waters – was a spectacular triumph, but the sinking of two barges was much more typical of the action to come.

The terrible attrition of ships in the Guadalcanal fight had left the Japanese short of sea transport. Besides, Allied airmen made the sea approaches to New Guinea a dangerous place for surface craft in daylight. Nevertheless, the Japanese had to find some way to supply their New Guinea beachheads by sea or give them up, so they began a crash program of barge construction.

The barges were of many types, but the most formidable was the *daihatsu*, a steel or wooden barge, diesel powered, armored, heavily armed with machine guns or even with automatic light cannon. They could not be torpedoed, because their draft was so shallow that a torpedo would pass harmlessly under their hulls. They could soak up enormous amounts of machine-gun fire and could strike back with their own automatic weapons and the weapons of soldier passengers. A single *daihatsu* could be a dangerous target for a PT. A fleet of *daihatsus*, giving each other mutual fire support, could well be too much to handle even for a brace of coordinated PTs.

The naval war around New Guinea became a nightly brawl between *daihatsu* and PT, and the torpedo function of the PT shriveled. Eventually many of the boats abandoned their torpedo tubes entirely and placed them with 37-mm. and 40-mm. cannon and extra 50-caliber machine guns, fine weapons for punching through a *daihatsu*'s armor. The PT in New Guinea gradually changed its main armament from the torpedo — a sledge-hammer type of weapon for battering heavy warships — to the multiple autocannon — a buzz-saw type of weapon for slicing up small craft.

At the Buna-Gona-Sananada battlefield, the Japanese were dying of starvation. It was the story of Guadalcanal again — with supply from the sea cut off by aggressive American patrols, the emperor's infantry — no matter how desperately brave — could not stand up to a long campaign.

The night between January 17th and 18th, the *Roaring Twenty* (PT 120) caught three barges trying to slip out of Sanananda. The PT recklessly took on all three in a machine-gun duel, sank two of them, and set the third afire. PT sailors were the first to know that the end had come for the Japanese ashore, because the barges were loaded with Japanese officers trying to slip away from their doomed men. Next day Sananada fell to the Australians.

When both the base at Sanananda, on the turkey's tail, and Guadalcanal fell to the Allies in the first months of 1943, the Japanese tried to slam an impenetrable gate across the path of the Allied advance. The eastern hinge of the gate was to be the mighty naval base and airfield complex at Rabaul, on the island of New Britain. The western hinge was planned for the place where the turkey's tail joins the turkey's back, an indentation of the New Guinea coastline called Huon Gulf.

To build up the western hinge of the gate, the Japanese landed at the ports of Lae, Salamaua, and Finschhafen, on the Huon Gulf. The Japanese wanted Huon Gulf so badly that they even dared send a fleet of surface transports to ferry 6,900 reinforcements across the Bismarck Sea to New Guinea. The convoy run was daring, because it would be within reach of land-based Allied bombers almost the whole way.

Escorting the eight transports were eight destroyers, veterans of the Tokyo Express. Tanaka, however, was no longer with them. He had been relieved of his command for telling the high navy brass in Tokyo some unpleasant truths. He spent the rest of the war on the beach as a penalty for speaking up about mistakes made at Guadalcanal.

The Japanese convoy sailed from Rabaul, at the eastern hinge of the gate, on March 1st, under cover of a terrible storm which the ships' captains hoped would ground Allied bombers. On March 3rd the storm lifted unexpectedly. The seasick soldiers felt slightly less miserable.

In Japan March 3rd is Doll's Day, a sentimental family holiday when little Japanese girls dress up their dolls and parade them about the streets under the fond eyes of admiring fathers. Many of the soldiers were depressed at being on such a martial mission on Doll's Day, so their officers passed out candy as a little touch of holiday. The officers did not tell the soldiers that the lifting of the storm had been a disaster, that an Allied snooper had already spotted the convoy, and that Allied bombers were almost surely on the way.

Worse was on the way than ordinary bombers. Back in Australia, the American bomber force had been working on a new dirty trick, and bomber pilots were eager to try it on the transports crowded with candy-munching soldiers.

Mechanics had torn out all the bombardier equipment from the nose of B 25 attack bombers and had mounted eight 50-caliber machine guns. Under each B 25 they had slung two 500-pound bombs armed with five-second delay fuses. The idea was to make a low-level bombing run, so as to skip the bombs across the water like flat stones. The delayed-action fuses were to keep the bombs from detonating until they had slammed into the ships' sides. When the snooper reported the convoy, it sounded to Allied bomber pilots like the perfect target for testing the new weapon.

While fighters and high-level bombers kept the Japanese convoy occupied, the converted B 25s came at the Japanese so low that the blast of their propellers churned the sea. The Japanese skippers thought they were torpedo bombers – which they were, in a sense – and turned into the attack, to present the narrowest possible target, a wise maneuver ordinarily, but this also made the ships the best possible targets for the long, thin pattern of the machine-gun ripsaws mounted in the bombers' noses. The ships were ripped from stem to gudgeon by the strafing runs. Then, when the pilots were sure the antiaircraft gun crews had been sawed to shreds, the low-flying B 25s charged at the ships broadside and released the skip bombs, which caved in hull plates at the waterlines and let in fatal doses of sea water. It was almost impossible to miss with a skip bomb. By nightfall the Bismarck Sea was dotted with rafts, lifeboats, and swimmers clinging to the debris of sunken ships. Only darkness stopped the slaughter from the air.

After that sunset, however, the slaughter from the sea became more grisly than ever. Eight PTs from New Guinea, under Lieut. Commander Barry K. Atkins, fought their way to the battle zone through the heavy seas in the wake of the storm which had so treacherously deserted the Japanese convoy.

Just before midnight they spotted the burning transport *Oigawa Maru*. PT 143 and PT 150 each fired a torpedo and blew the transport out of the water. The PT sailors searched all night but could find no other targets—largely because almost all of them were already on the floor of the Bismarck Sea.

When the sun came up they had targets enough, but of a most distasteful kind. The sea was swarming with Japanese survivors, and it was the unhappy duty of the PTs to try to kill them to the last man, so that they could not get ashore on nearby New Guinea.

On March 5th the same two PTs that had sunk the *Oigawa Maru* jumped a Japanese submarine picking up survivors from three boats. The PTs charged, firing torpedoes, but they missed the crash-diving submarine. Then they were presented with the hideous problem of what to do with the

100 helpless soldiers who watched fearfully from the three boats. The Japanese would not surrender, and they could not be allowed to escape.

The two PTs turned on the machine guns and set about the grim butchery of the unhappy Japanese. When the execution was over, they sank the three blood-drenched boats with a shallow pattern of depth charges.

Scout planes conned other PTs to lifeboats and rafts crammed with Japanese. More than 3,000 soldiers died, but so thick were the survivors that several hundred managed to swim ashore despite the best vigilance of the small-craft navy. The natives of New Guinea, who had long chafed against the Australian law forbidding head-hunting, were unleashed by the authorities and had a field day tracking down the few Japanese who made it to the beach.

Eighteen Japanese made an astonishing 400-mile voyage through PT-patrolled waters to a tiny island in the Trobriand group. They were captured by the crew of PT 114 in a pioneer landing party operation of the PT fleet.

The skip bombers of the American Air Force had sunk four destroyers and eight transports, killed 3,000 Japanese soldiers and sailors, and shot down 30 planes. The Battle of the Bismarck Sea was a smashing blow to the Japanese, and they never again risked a surface transport near eastern New

Guinea (except for a one-night run of four destroyers in a feeble and abortive attempt to set up a spurline of the Tokyo Express.)

The American Navy had an official torpedo-boat doctrine, of course, and PT officers were well drilled in the proper manner of delivering torpedoes in combat before they left the States, but this night-prowling business against torpedo-proof barges called for new torpedo-boat tactics.

Lieuts. (jg) Skipper Dean in PT 114, and Francis H. McAdoo, Jr., in PT 129, tried the still-hunt methods of Mississippi, where sportsmen hide themselves beside a known game trail and let the stag walk right up to his death. On the night between March 15th and 16th, the two PTs set up an ambush in a known barge rendezvous. They slipped into Mai-Ama Bay, a tiny inlet on the Huon Gulf shoreline, which they suspected was a Japanese barge terminal, and there they cut their engines and waited. As usual, it was raining and visibility was virtually zero.

The current persisted in setting the boats toward the gulf, so the 114 dropped anchor. Lieut. McAdoo found that he was too restless for a still hunt, so he oozed the 129 back into the gulf on one engine, to see if any barges were unloading south of the entrance to the bay.

The PT sailors didn't know it, but six Japanese barges had arrived before them and were unloading all around in the darkness. Two of the drifting barges, already unloaded and idling about the bay until time to form up for the return trip, bumped into the side of the 114. To the PT sailors it was as though a clammy hand had touched them in a haunted house. They were galvanized.

Silence and stealth were second nature to them, however, so they moved quietly to battle stations. The Japanese on the barges, happily assuming that the PT was another Japanese ship, chattered amiably among themselves.

Machine-gunners on the PT strained to depress their 50-caliber mounts, but the barges were too close. Sailors quietly cocked submachine guns instead.

At the skipper's signal, with blazing Tommy guns, the crew hosed down the decks of the two *daihatsus* that were holding the PT in their embarrassingly close embrace. The PT anchor was snagged to the bottom, so a sailor parted the line with an ax, and the PT tried to put a little distance between itself and the Japanese.

The aft 50 calibers sank one barge, but the other caught under the bow of the PT and plugged its escape route. Skipper Dean solved the problem by shoving the throttles up to the stops and riding over the barge, which swamped and sank under the PT's weight.

The 114, once free from the two *daihatsus*,

turned back into the inlet with guns roaring. The 129 came running, and the two PTs mopped up the rest of the six-barge convoy.

The Australian army had taken on the job of throwing the Japanese out of the three Huon Gulf villages that formed the western hinge of the Japanese gate. They were doing as well as could be expected with the nasty job of fighting in the filthy jungles of New Guinea, but they were having supply problems almost as serious as those of the blockaded Japanese. The Allies had no beachhead near the Australians, and supplies, in miserly quantities, had to be flown to a jungle airstrip and packed to the troops by native bearers.

The PT fleet in New Guinea had become so sophisticated by this time that it had acquired a formal organization and an over-all commander, a former submarine skipper named Morton Mumma. Aboard one of his PTs, Commander Mumma had gone poking about the little-known shoreline around the Huon Gulf (Mort Bay was named for him, because he first explored it), and he had found a fine landing beach at Nassau Bay. The beach was right under the nose of the Japanese garrison at Salamaua, it's true, but it was also temptingly handy to the Australian lines.

On the last day of June, 1943, three PTs packed a company of riflemen on their deck. With 36 small Army landing boats, the PTs sortied into a foul sea, lashed by high winds and rain. Total naval escort for the amphibious armada was PT 168, which presumably was in better fighting trim than the others, because it carried no seasick passengers. PT 168 promptly lost its convoy in the storm.

The Flying Shamrock (PT 142) missed the landing beach at Nassau Bay and did a countermarch. In the rain and darkness, the *Shamrock* beat the astronomical odds against such an accident by ramming the tiny PT 143, to the alarm of the miserable foot soldiers on both boats.

The Army landing craft scattered in the storm, and the two PTs had to round them up and guide them to the beach, where several broached in the high surf and were abandoned. Short of landing craft to put their own sea-weary passengers ashore, the PTs had to carry them back to the staging area.

Despite the less than 100 per cent efficiency of the operation, the few American soldiers who had reached the beach threw the Japanese garrison into a panic. A lucky bomb hit had killed their able commander, and without his support the 300 Japanese assigned to guard Nassau Bay broke and fled before the insignificant Allied invasion force.

Puny as they were, the landings at Nassau Bay threw the Japanese high command into a flap.

They saw clearly, possibly even more clearly than the Allies, that the Nassau Bay beachhead was going to unhinge the whole Japanese gate across the Allied path. The landings also paid an unexpected bonus far to the east, where American soldiers were landing on Rendova Island, as part of the island-hopping advance up the central Solomons toward the eastern hinge of the Japanese gate. The Japanese at Rabaul were so alarmed by the minuscule PT operation at Nassau Bay that they jammed their own radio circuits with alarms and outcries. The Japanese at Rendova couldn't get anybody to listen to their anguished cries for help, and the American troops went ashore with almost no air opposition.

Ashore on Huon Gulf, the Australians still had the uncomfortable job of convincing the stubborn Japanese foot soldiers that they were doomed, and previously the only way to convince them had been to kill them by bullets or starvation. The PTs tightened the blockade by night.

Just before the end at Finschhafen, when the Japanese were getting ready to give up the Huon Gulf, barge traffic increased. It was the same story as the earlier abandonment of Buna, Gona, and Sananda. The Japanese were slipping out by night.

On the night between August 28th and 29th, two PTs patrolled off Finschhafen. Ensign Herbert P. Knight was skipper of the 152; Lieut. (jg) John

L. Carey was skipper of *The Flying Shamrock* (PT 142). Riding the *Shamrock*, in command of the operation, was a most distinguished PT sailor, Lieut. John Bulkeley, rescuer of MacArthur, back from his tour in the United States as the number one naval hero of the Philippines campaign.

Lookouts spotted three barges, and one went down under the first attack by the two PT boats, but the other two were still afloat after the third firing run. Ensign Knight dropped depth charges alongside, but the barges rode out the blast and were still afloat when the geysers of sea water settled. Lieut. Carey made a depth-charge run and blew one of the barges apart, but the other still survived.

Aboard the *Shamrock*, Bulkeley decided to finish the job in the old-fashioned way — by hand.

For the first time in this century, with a cry of "Boarders away," a U. S. Navy boarding party, weapons in hand, swarmed aboard an enemy craft. One Japanese made a move in the darkness, and Lieut. Bulkeley blew him down with a 45 automatic. The other passengers, twelve fully equipped soldiers, were already dead.

The boarders picked up what documents and equipment they thought would be interesting to Intelligence, and reboarded their PT. The 152 pumped 37-mm shells into the barge until it slid under the water.

Ashore, Intelligence captured the diary of a Japanese officer named Kobayashi. Under the date of August 29, 1943, was the entry:

> Last night with the utmost precaution we were without incident transported safely by barge between Sio and Finschhafen. *So far, there has not been a time during such trips when barges have not been attacked by enemy torpedo boats.* However, it was reported that the barge unit which transported us was attacked and sunk on the return trip last night and the barge commander and his men were all lost.

The PT blockade at sea and the Australian drive ashore pinched the Japanese hard, and on September 16th Australian infantrymen walked into a deserted Finschhafen. The western hinge of the gate had been broken.

4.

Battering Down the Gate:

the Eastern Hinge

THE WESTERN END of the Japanese gate was nailed to the great land mass of New Guinea, and its unhinging was a natural job for the Army. The eastern hinge was at Rabaul, in the tangle of islands and reef-strewn sea channels that make up the Solomon and Bismarck archipelagos. Reduction of Rabaul was naturally a Navy job, to be carried on simultaneously with the Army effort in New Guinea.

After the fall of Guadalcanal in February, 1943, the master plan in the South Pacific, under Admiral William Halsey, was to hop from island to island through the central Solomons, reducing one by one the Japanese bases arranged like steppingstones between Guadalcanal and Rabaul.

PTs were moved up as fast as new bases were established, because they were short of range and useless if they fell too far behind the front.

The night the Army went ashore at Rendova (June 30, 1943), three PTs sailed up Blanche Channel, on the approaches to the Rendova landing beach. Coming down the same channel was the American landing flotilla, transports, supply ships, and escorting destroyers. The destroyer *McCawley*, damaged by one of the few Japanese air attacks that opposed the Rendova landings, was being towed to Tulagi, but was riding lower and lower in the water and its survival was doubtful. Rear Admiral Richmond K. Turner (riding *McCawley* as flagship of the Rendova invasion force) was debating whether or not to give the stricken ship euthanasia by friendly torpedo when his mind was made up for him by two mysterious fish which came out of the night and blew *McCawley* out of the water.

The deadly PTs had struck again! But, alas, under the illusion that they were hitting an enemy transport. Explanation of the snafu? The usual lack of communications between PTs and other commands. The PTs had been told there would be no friendlies in Blanche Channel that night—and the only friendlies they encountered just happened to be the entire Rendova landing fleet.

American soldiers quickly captured Rendova Island, and the PT navy set up a base there. Across Blanche Channel, on New Georgia Island, Marines and soldiers were fighting a heartbreaking jungle action to capture the Japanese airfield at Munda, but they had taken over enough of New

Georgia for another PT base on The Slot side of the island.

Business was slow at first for the PTs. The big-ship admirals, who were fighting repeated destroyer-cruiser night actions in those waters — and who were possibly nervous about the PTs since the *McCawley* incident — ordered the PTs to stay in when the big ships went out.

Concern of the admirals over poor communications between PTs and other units was justified. Early on the morning of July 20th, three torpedo boats were returning to Rendova Base through Fergusson Passage. Three B 25s—the same kind of aircraft that had performed such terrible execution of the Japanese in the Bismarck Sea — spotted the patrol craft and came down to the deck for a strafing run.

Aboard PT 168, Lieut. Edward Macauley III held his gunners in tight check while they suffered under the murderous fire of the friendly planes. Repeatedly the gunners of the 168 held their breath as the B 25s raked them with bullets — but they held their own fire in a superb display of discipline. Not so the other two boats. Gunners were unable to stand being shot at without shooting back, and the first PT burst of counterfire brought down a bomber in flames.

Somehow the other bombers came to their senses and the strafing runs stopped, but all the boats had already been riddled and two were burning. The 166 was past saving. Sound crew members helped the wounded over the side into life rafts and paddled frantically away from the burning craft. They made it out of danger just as the gas tanks went up in a blast of searing orange flame.

Lieut. Macauley and his brave crew – the only group to come out of the ghastly affair with unblemished credit–took their still burning 168 alongside the stricken bomber to rescue survivors before the plane went down. Three of the bomber crew were dead; the three survivors were wounded. One bomber and one PT were lost in the sad affair. One officer and ten men of the torpedo-boat patrol were wounded.

Reason for the tragic mistake? Same as for the *McCawley* sinking. The bomber pilots had been told that there would be no friendly vessels in those waters at that time.

PTs were harassed, during the night patrols, by Japanese seaplanes escorting the Japanese barge convoys, so one PT skipper and a night fighter plane rigged an ambush. An American night fighter was to perch aloft, the PT was to charge about, throwing up a glittering rooster's tail of a wake to attract a float plane, and the night fighter was to jump on the float plane's back.

The plan worked like a fifty-dollar clock. The

noisy, rambunctious PT lured down a float plane – OK so far – and the PT's skipper conned the escorting night fighter in to the counterattack.

The first word from the night fighter, however, was a disconcerting, "I'm being attacked by the float plane."

"Bring him down to two feet," said the PT skipper, "and *we'll* get on his tail."

Nobody was hurt.

PTs fought some lively barge actions on July 23rd and 27th, but the big battle – the naval battle which has earned what is surely the most exaggerated fame of all time for its importance – the battle of the 109, took place the night between August 1st and 2nd.

On the afternoon of August 1st, search planes saw four Japanese destroyers coming down The Slot. They were loaded with 900 soldiers and supplies for the embattled defenders of the Munda airfield. It was a typical run of the Tokyo Express and a prime target for PTs.

During the afternoon, when the Japanese destroyers were still far from Rendova, the Japanese showed their deep respect for motor torpedo boats by socking the Rendova base with bombs from 25 planes.

Two PTs were sunk by a bomber which crashed into their nest. One of the PTs destroyed was

164, which had survived the tragic strafing by B25s just eleven days before.

At sunset 15 PTs — four of them equipped with the new-fangled gadget called radar — sortied from the base under the command of Lieut. Henry J. Brantingham aboard 159. Brantingham was another veteran of the MacArthur rescue run in the Philippines. The PTs were deployed around the approaches to the Japanese landing beach for resupplying Munda airfield.

Lieut. Brantingham, naturally, had chosen a radar-equipped boat for his flagship, and so was the first to pick up the Tokyo Express, just after midnight on August 2nd. Brantingham, for some reason, thought his radar pips were from landing craft, and closed for a strafing run, but 4.7-inch shells from the destroyers persuaded him that his targets were fair torpedo game. He and Lieut. (jg) William F. Liebnow, Jr., in 157, fired six torpedoes. No hits. The two boats escaped behind puffs of smoke.

Worse than the six misses was the lack of communication. The other PTs, most of them without radar, didn't even know the destroyers had arrived on the scene, much less that they had been alerted by the torpedo runs of 157 and 159.

Next to pick up the cans was the radar-equipped 171, carrying the division commander, Lieut. Arthur H. Berndtson. The boat's skipper,

Ensign William Cullen Battle, closed at a slinking ten knots to 1,500 yards, where Lieut. Berndtson fired a full salvo of fish. All four tubes blazed up in a grease fire that was as helpful to the destroyer gunners as a spotlighted bull's-eye. Shellbursts splashed water aboard the 171 as the boat ripped out to sea.

Again the attacking PT which had missed its target failed to report by radio to the other PT skippers, who were straining their eyes in the darkness looking for ships they didn't know were already on the scene.

A third radar boat, Lieut. George E. Cookman's 107, picked up the cans on the radar set and missed with four fish. Three other PTs, aroused by the flash of destroyer gunfire, came running from the southeast. A Japanese float plane strafed them, and destroyer salvos straddled the boats, but they got off all their torpedoes – 12 of them – and all 12 missed.

The Tokyo Express went through the strait and unloaded 900 soldiers and supplies.

So bad were communications between the PTs that most of the 15 skippers who had started the patrol still didn't know that the destroyers had arrived and been unsuccessfully attacked, much less that they had already discharged their cargoes and were going home. And that meant the destroyers were coming up on the PT lookouts from behind.

At the wheel of the 109 was Lieut. John F. Kennedy. The boat was idling along on one engine to save fuel and to cruise as silently as possible — good PT doctrine for night patrol.

A lookout on the destroyer *Amagiri* saw the 109 at about the same instant a lookout on the PT saw the destroyer. Making a split-second decision, Japanese Commander Hanami ordered the helmsman to spin the wheel to starboard and ram.

The *Amagiri* crashed into the starboard side of the 109 and killed the lookout on the spot. The boat was cut in two; the rear section sank; burning gasoline covered the sea. The *Amagiri* sailed on, but at a reduced speed, because the 109, in its death agony, had bent vanes on the *Amagiri's* starboard propeller, causing violent vibration at high speeds.

PT 169 fired torpedoes at the *Amagiri,* but at too close a range for them to arm and explode. PT 157 fired two that missed. Thirty torpedoes were fired that night, and the only damage inflicted on the destroyers was by the quite involuntary and fatal body block of the 109. It was not the greatest night of the war for the PT navy.

Eleven survivors of the 109 searched surrounding waters for two missing shipmates, but never found them. They spent the night and the next morning on the still-floating bow section. By midafternoon they decided that no rescue was on the way. Since they felt naked and exposed to Japanese plane and ship patrols, they set out to swim three and a half miles to a desert island, the skipper towing a badly burned shipmate for four hours by a life-jacket tie-tie gripped between his teeth.

After harrowing nights spent on several desert islands — nights during which the skipper showed most extraordinary stamina, resourcefulness, and courage — the ship-wrecked sailors were found by native scouts. They took the heroic skipper by canoe to a coast-watcher station, and there he boarded a rescue PT and returned for his marooned companions.

The skipper of the 109 was, of course, the same John F. Kennedy who on January 20, 1961, became the thirty-fifth President of the United States.

After Munda fell and with it all of New Georgia, American strategists studied the map and decided that island-by-island reduction of Japanese strength was too tedious. They decided to start by-passing some of the bases, cutting off the by-passed garrisons and starving them behind an American sea blockade. More night work for the PTs.

Up the line a bit was the island of Vella Lavella, only lightly held by the Japanese. American strategists chose a beach called Barakoma as a possible landing spot and ordered a reconnaissance.

Four PTs, on the night between August 12th and 13th, carried a scouting party of 45 men to the beach at Barakoma. A Japanese plane nagged the boats with strafing and bombing runs for two hours. A near miss tore up the planking on the 168 and wounded four sailors, so the 168 had to drop out of the operation, but the other three boats put their passengers ashore safely. Scouts reported that the only Japanese around that part of the island were ship-wrecked survivors of an earlier sea battle, so thirty-six hours later four more PTs landed reinforcements.

Japanese snooper planes spotted the PT passenger runs, but apparently the Japanese high command couldn't think of torpedo boats as invasion craft, so the scout landings were made without interference.

The main force followed, and by October 1st all of Vella Lavella was in American hands.

The Japanese began shrinking their Solomon Islands perimeter, falling back to the islands on the near side of the new American base at Vella Lavella. American destroyers, out to smash the evacuation bargeline, met a Japanese destroyer screen for the *daihatsus* on the night between October 6th and 7th. As usual, Japanese torpedoes were deadly. One American destroyer went down and two others were sorely damaged. More important, the Japanese supply and evacuation train ran its errands without molestation from the American cans.

The American destroyers did sink the Japanese *Yugumo*, and American PTs were sent to pick up 78 survivors. Aboard the 163, an American sailor offered a cup of coffee to one of the captive Japanese, who killed the Good Samaritan (and of course died himself at the hands of the murdered sailor's shipmates). PT sailors felt less uneasy about the massacre of the shipwrecked Japanese at the Bismarck Sea after the treacherous murder of their comrade by a rescued Japanese.

Having successfully leapfrogged once, American strategists looked at the map again. The whole point to the island-hopping campaign was to put American fighter planes close enough to Rabaul so that they could screen bombers over that base and keep the Japanese pinned down there under constant bombardment. The best site for a fighter base was Bougainville Island, so American planners put their fingers on the map and said: "This is the place for the next one."

Accordingly, Marines landed at Cape Torokina, on Bougainville, on November 1st. Their mission was to capture enough of the island to build and protect a fighter strip. The rest of the island could be left to the 15,000 Japanese soldiers who defended it. Nobody cared about them. Rabaul was the real target.

The Japanese high command at Rabaul sent down a cruiser-destroyer force with the mission of getting among the American transports in Empress Augusta Bay, off Torokina, and tearing up the helpless train ships like a pack of wolves in a herd of sheep.

An American cruiser-destroyer force met them just after midnight on November 2nd, and sank one Japanese cruiser and a destroyer. More important, the American flotilla ran off the Japanese marauders before they reached the transports.

American reconnaissance planes, however, spotted a massive concentration of heavy cruisers and destroyers building up in Rabaul Harbor, a concentration too great for American naval forces then in the South Pacific to handle, because most American capital ships of the Pacific Fleet had been pulled back toward Hawaii to support an operation in the Gilbert Islands.

Admiral Halsey scratched together a carrier task force, and even though a carrier raid near a land-based airfield was then against doctrine, he sent the carrier's planes into the harbor. They damaged the cruisers badly enough to relieve the immediate threat to the Torokina landings. The carrier raids stirred up a hornet's nest around Rabaul.

Eighteen Japanese torpedo bombers took off to smash the brazen carrier task force. Just before total dark they found American ships and attacked. Radio Tokyo broadcast, with jubilation, that the score in this "First Air Battle of Bougainville" was "one large carrier blown up and sunk, one medium carrier set ablaze and later sunk, and two heavy cruisers and one cruiser and destroyer sunk." Rabaul's torpedo bombers won a group commendation.

An American staff officer, hearing the account of this First Air Battle of Bougainville as reported by Japanese pilots, could only hold his head in his hands and hope his own pilots were not feeding him the same kind of foolishness.

Here is what really happened in the First Air Battle of Bougainville.

A landing craft, the LCI 70, and the PT 167, were lumbering back from a landing party on the Torokina beachhead. Just after sunset the Japanese bombers struck in low-level torpedo runs. The PT brought down the leader by the novel method of snagging him with its mast. The plane's torpedo punched clean through the PT's nose, leaving its tail assembly, appropriately enough, in the crew's head.

The torpedo boat's 20-mm. cannon shot down a second torpedo bomber so close to the ship that the sailors on the fantail were soaked.

Four torpedo bombers launched their fish at the LCI, but since the torpedoes were set for attack on a deep-draft carrier, they passed harmlessly under the landing craft's shallow hull – except for one which porpoised and jumped through the LCI's thin skin, unfortunately killing one sailor. The unexploded warhead came to rest on a starchy bed in the bread locker. The torpedo was still smoking, so the LCI's skipper, Lieut. (jg) H. W. Frey, ordered "Abandon ship!"

Time passed. No explosion. A damage-control party reboarded the LCI and rigged her for a tow back to Torokina. PT 167 raced ahead with the wounded.

Rear Admiral T. S. Wilkinson radioed congratulations to Ensign Theodore Berlin, skipper of the PT, for knocking down a plane with his mast. "Fireplug sprinkles dog," is the way the admiral put it.

So ended the First Air Battle of Bougainville.

PTs quickly set up a base on Puruata Island, just off the Torokina beachhead, even though the Marine foothold was still feeble. Sea patrols of the torpedo boats were still vexed by poor communications. The night of November 8th, for instance, the destroyers *Hudson* and *Anthony* came up to Torokina, sure that there were no friendly PTs in the bay, because higher-ups on the beach had told them so. Naturally, when radar picked up the pips of patrolling PTs 163, 169 and 170, they let fly with everything.

The PTs, equally misinformed about what friendlies to expect, took the destroyer broadsides to be a most unfriendly action and maneuvered for a torpedo run. The skipper of the 170 tried to decoy the two American destroyers into a trap. He called the 163 by radio, to warn him that he was leading "three Nip cans" into their torpedo range. PT 163 got off a long shot at the "three" cans, which fortunately missed.

There has been much fruitless speculation about that third mysterious can reported by 170. Aboard the 170, the radar screen showed a big target – not one of the two American destroyers – 10,000 yards dead ahead. A salvo of shells that "looked like ashcans" passed overhead, coming from the same direction as the radar target. To this day nobody knows who was the assailant with guns big enough to fire ashcan-sized projectiles.

The running duel lit up the bay for forty-five minutes. The torpedo boats were just coming around for a new torpedo run when *Anthony* figured out what was going on.

"Humblest apologies," the *Anthony* said by radio in a handsome bid to accept all the blame. "We are friendly vessels."

Farther west near Arawe, on New Britain, on

Christmas Day 1943, Lieut. Ed Farley's 190, with Lieut. Commander H. M. S. Swift aboard, and Ensign Rumsey Ewing's 191 were returning to the Dregar Harbor base in New Guinea, after a dull patrol.

Between 30 and 38 Japanese dive bombers and fighters came down from the north and bombed and strafed the boats in groups of three and four. The two little PTs were in a jam, for the force attacking them was large enough to take on a carrier task force, screen destroyers and all. The boats separated, went to top speed, and zigzagged toward a bank of low clouds twelve miles away.

Japanese planes often made one pass at PTs and then dropped the job if they did not score, but this overwhelming big flight of planes returned for repeated attacks. PT skippers clamored for fighter cover from the beach.

Aboard the 191, the skipper was hit in the lungs and Ensign Fred Calhoun took command. A machine-gun bullet pierced his thigh, but he hung on to the wheel to play a deadly game of tag with the attackers. He held a steady course, his eye fixed to the bomb racks of the attacking plane, until the bomb was away and committed to its course. Then he whipped over the wheel to put the boat where the bomb wasn't when it landed.

Nevertheless, fragments from a near miss knocked out a 20-mm. gun and severely wounded the gunner, Chief Motor Machinist Mate Thomas Dean, and the loader, Motor Machinist Mate Second Class August Sciutto. Another near miss punched an 18-inch hole in the portside and peppered the superstructure with steel splinters.

Japanese strafers hit the port and starboard engines and punctured the water jackets, which spurted jets of boiling water into the engine room. Engineer of the Watch Victor Bloom waded into the streams of scalding water to tape and stuff leaks so that the engines would not overheat and fuse into a solid mass.

Fearing that the gas fumes from punctured lines might explode, he closed off the fuel-tank compartment and pulled a release valve to smother it with carbon dioxide. When he had tidied up his engine room, Bloom gave first aid to the wounded. (Not surprisingly, Victor Bloom won a Navy Cross for this action.)

By this time the two PTs had knocked four planes into the sea near the boats.

"Toward the end of the attack," said Lieut. Farley, "the enemy became more and more inaccurate and less willing to close us. It is possible that we may have knocked down the squadron leader as the planes milled about in considerable confusion, as if lacking leadership."

Forty minutes after they were called, P 47 fighter planes from Finschhafen arrived to drive off the shaken Japanese apparently startled by the two floating buzz saws.

One of the P 47s was hit and made a belly landing about half a mile from the 190. The pilot, though badly wounded in the head and arm, freed himself and escaped from the cockpit before his plane went down. The 190 went to the rescue of its rescuer, and Lieut. Commander Swift and Seaman First Class Joe Cope jumped overboard to tow the groggy pilot to the undamaged PT.

Authorities were as astonished as the Japanese attackers had been by the savage and effective response of the two PTs to the massive attack which should have wiped them out, according to all the rules. Smaller and less determined air attacks had sunk cruisers and destroyers in other waters.

Commander Mumma, with justifiable pride in his two boats, said of the action: "It has shown that the automatic weapon armament is most effective. It has demonstrated that ably handled PTs can, in daylight, withstand heavy air attack."

On the same Christmas Day 1943, the Bougainville bomber strip went into business, and the fighter strips were so well established that American forces could afford to settle down behind the barbed wire of The Perimeter, content with what they already held. From here on out, they could afford to ignore as much as possible the 15,000

Japanese still on the island. From that day Rabaul was doomed to comparative impotence under a merciless shower of bombs.

Not that Rabaul was a feeble outpost. One hundred thousand Japanese soldiers, behind powerful fortifications and with immense supplies, made Rabaul a formidable fortress — too tough for a direct frontal assault — until the end of the war. Without air power, however, the Japanese there could do nothing to hold back the Allied advance except to glower at the task forces passing by just out of gun range on their way to new island bases farther up the line.

The Japanese gate was unhinged at both ends and the Allies poured through the gap.

American strategists decided to jump over Rabaul, leaving its defenders to shrivel away behind a sea blockade. Some of the PTs leapfrogged with the rest of the Allied forces and readied for more night patrol in the waters farther along the sea lanes to Tokyo; some of them stayed behind to make life as miserable as possible for the bypassed Japanese on Bougainville and the other islands cut off from home.

PTs played a big part in the last jump that isolated Rabaul. The landings in the Admiralty Islands were on Leap Year Day, February 29, 1944, by units of the First Cavalry Division. The

Admiralty Islands are a ring of long, thin islands enclosing a magnificent anchorage called Seeadler Harbor. The fine anchorage and the airstrips planned for the islands would give the Allies the last brick in the wall around Rabaul.

Faulty reconnaissance from the air had shown that the islands were free of Japanese. Actually there were 4,000 Japanese in the islands, and their commander was insulted that the Americans landed a force only a fraction the size of his. He counterattacked violently. The only Navy fire support available was from destroyers and small craft.

Among the small craft were MTB Squadron Twenty-One, commanded by Lieutenant Paul Rennell, and Squadron Eighteen, commanded by the same Lieut. Commander H. M. S. Swift who had surprised the Japanese air command by the vicious antiaircraft fire of his two torpedo boats near Arawe on Christmas Day.

The PTs went to work for the cavalry as a kind of sea cavalry, running errands, carrying wounded, towing stranded boats off the beach, handling the leadline to measure a poorly charted harbor bottom, and even carrying cavalry generals on scouting missions.

From inside Seeadler Harbor they gave the cavalry close fire support with machine guns and mortars. A keen-eyed sailor on 363 knocked a sniper out of a tree with a short burst, for instance, and the crew of the 323 demolished, with 50 calibers, a Japanese radio and observation platform in another tree.

The island of Manus fell quickly, and Major General I. P. Swift, commanding general of the First Cavalry Division, in a generous tribute to a sister service, said: "The bald statement, 'The naval forces supported this action' . . . is indeed a masterpiece of understatement. . . . Without the Navy there would not have been any action."

5.

Along the Turkey's Back

FROM THE TIME that American planes stopped the Japanese onrush at the Coral Sea and at Midway, it was a two-year job for the Allies to batter down the Japanese gate at Rabaul and at the Huon Gulf. Once the gate was down, it took MacArthur's forces only four months to make the 1,200-mile trip down the turkey's back to a perch on the turkey's head, just across from the East Indies and the Philippines.

The swift trip was made possible, however, by a leap-frogging technique that left behind a monumental job for the PT navy. General MacArthur made almost all of his New Guinea landings where the Japanese weren't, by-passing tens of thousands of tough jungle fighters and leaving the job of starving them out to the blockading navy. Except for the brief loan of ships from the battleline for special missions, the blockading navy was the PT fleet.

The New Guinea PT force was beefed up for the blockade by many new boats and officers. Mac-

Arthur had been deeply impressed by the torpedo boats during his escape from Corregidor and used all his influence — which was considerable in those days — to impress every PT possible into his force.

The PTs in New Guinea lost almost all use for their torpedoes, except when they chanced to catch a blockade-running supply submarine on the surface. The boat skippers wanted more guns, more auto-cannon and machine guns for shooting up the Number One blockade-runner, the armored *daihatsu* — and they got them.

Early in November 1943, Squadron Twenty-One arrived at Morobe base armed with 40-mm. auto-cannon, a tremendously effective weapon for all-around mischief. It was the first New Guinea squadron armed with the newer and deadlier weapon.

More than the size of the new cannon, however, the size of the new officers astonished the veteran PT sailors. Commander Selman S. Bowling, who had replaced Commander Mumma as chief of PTs in the Southwest Pacific, had voluntarily ridden on the Tulagi boats before his new assignment, and he had decided then that PT officers should be tough and athletic. When he went to the States to organize new squadrons, he had recruited the biggest, toughest athletes he could find.

Among the newcomers were Ensign Ernest

W. Pannell, All-American tackle from Texas A. and M. and professional football player for the Green Bay Packers; Ensign Alex Schibanoff of Franklin and Marshall College and the Detroit Lions; Ensign Steven L. Levanitis of Boston College and the Philadelphia Eagles; Ensign Bernard A. Crimmins, All-American from Notre Dame; Lieut. (jg) Paul B. Lillis, captain of the Notre Dame team; Ensign Louis E. Smith, University of California halfback; Ensign Kermit W. Montz, Franklin and Marshall; Ensign John M. Eastham, Jr., Texas A. and M.; Ensign Stuart A. Lewis, University of California; Ensign Cedric J. Janien, Harvard; and Ensign William P. Hall, Wabash.

Also bulging with muscle were Ensign Joseph W. Burk, holding the world's record as single-sculls champion; Ensign Kenneth D. Molloy, All-American lacrosse player from Syracuse University; Lieut. John B. Williams, Olympic swimmer from Oregon State; and Ensign James F. Foran, swimmer from Princeton.

Commander Bowling was right. PT crews had to be tough for the kind of warfare they were waging. Shallow-draft *daihatsus* clung to the shore, and the PTs had to come in as close as 100 yards from the beach to find their prey. For 1,200 miles the shoreline was lined with ten of thousands of blockaded Japanese soldiers, every one of them itching to get a crack at the patrol boats that were starving them to death. The Japanese set up shore batteries and baited traps with helpless-looking *daihatsus* to lure the PT marauders within range. In this deadly cat-and-mouse game, the PT did not always win.

About 2 A.M. on March 7th, PTs 337 and 338 slipped into Hansa Bay, a powerfully garrisoned Japanese base by-passed early in the Allied forward movement. The PTs poked about the enemy harbor and picked up a radar target close to shore. From 400 yards away, the two skippers saw that their radar pip came from two heavily camouflaged luggers moored together, a prime bit of business for PTs. Before they could open fire, however, they discovered that they had been baited into an amubsh.

Machine guns opened up on the beach, and the PTs returned the fire, but the best they could do was to strafe the bush at random, because the Japanese gun positions were well concealed.

The machine guns at close range were bad enough, but the PT crews "pulled 20 Gs" when a heavy battery began firing from the mouth of the bay. The PTs, already deep inside the bay, would have to pass close to the heavy guns to escape from the harbor. The worst was that the gunners were obviously crack artillerymen, for the first shell hit so close to the port bow of the 337 that water from the spout sluiced down the decks and shrapnel whizzed overhead.

The sharpshooting gunners of the shore battery put a shell from the next salvo into the tank compartment below the port turret. All engines went dead and the boat burst into flame. The skipper, Ensign Henry W. Cutter, pulled the CO_2 release valve but it was too late — the boat was doomed.

Francis C. Watson, Motor Machinist Mate, Third Class, who had been blown from the port turret by the shell blast, got to his feet and started forward, away from the searing flames, but he turned back into the fire to help William Daley, Jr., who was crawling painfully out of the burning engine room. Daley had been badly wounded in the neck and jaw. Watson pulled Daley from the flames and with Morgan J. Canterbury, Torpedomen's Mate, Second Class, carried him forward. Ensign Cutter put a life raft into the water on the side away from the big guns, and Daley, dazed but obedient, tried to get into the raft, but slipped overboard. The skipper and Ensign Robert W. Hyde jumped after him and towed him to the raft.

The crew paddled and pushed the raft away from the burning boat and out to sea, but a strong current worked against them and in two hours they made only 700 yards. When their boat exploded, the concussion hurt.

Searchlights swept the bay and guns fired all

night at the 338, which had escaped behind smoke and was now trying to get back *into* the death-trap to find out what had happened to their comrades of the 337. The crack gunners ashore were too good, however, and repeated brackets from heavy salvos kept the 338 outside until the rising sun drove the worried sailors home.

Daley died before sunrise, and — in the formal language of the Navy report — "was committed to the sea."

Survivors clinging to the three-by-seven-foot balsa oval were the skipper and Ensign Hyde, Watson, Canterbury; Ensign Bruce S. Bales; Allen B. Gregory, QM2c; Harry E. Barnett, RM2c; Henry S. Timmons, Y2c; Edgar L. Schmidt, TM3c; Evo A. Fucili, MoMM3c; and James P. Mitchell, SC3c.

The raft was not built for an 11-man load, so the sailors took turns riding in the slat-bottom craft and swimming alongside. Currents nagged them, and at dawn the raft was still less than a mile off the entrance to the bay, within easy reach of Japanese patrol boats.

During the morning the currents set the boat toward Manam Island, six miles away, and Ensign Cutter decided to make for the island, with the idea that he and his crew would hide in the woods. Maybe they would find food, water, shelter — who knows, just possibly a native canoe or sailboat.

All afternoon the sailors paddled for the island,

but the devilish currents were not through with them. Every time they came close to the beach a current would sweep them out to sea again.

Floating on the same currents were two logs which the sailors tied to the raft. After dark the skipper, still hopeful of finding a boat on the island, set out with Ensign Bales to swim to the beach, using the logs as a crude substitute for water wings. For three hours the two young officers swam, only to bump gently against their own raft again. The currents had carried them in a giant circle, back to their starting point.

Hyde and Gregory, tired of inaction, set out for the beach. They were never seen again.

That night the sailors watched the flash of gunfire at Hansa Bay, where their squadron mates shot up the beach in revenge for their loss. No PTs came close enough for the shipwrecked sailors to hail.

By their very nature, PT sailors were men of action. Their solution to any problem was, "Don't just sit there, *do* something." The inactivity of waiting passively for rescue was too much for some of them.

Just before dawn Mitchell set out for the island, and just after dawn Ensign Bales, Fucili, Watson, and Schmidt followed. The others would have gone, too, but they were too weak.

Watson returned to the raft in the middle of the morning. He had swum to within 75 yards of the shore, he said, and he had seen Ensign Bales walking around on dry land, but he had also seen Japanese workmen building boats in a shipyard, so he came back to the raft. All hands abandoned the idea of going to the island. After the war, captured documents showed that the Japanese on Manam Island had captured one officer and two enlisted men of the sailors who had swum ashore, but these three luckless sailors were never heard of after this brief mention.

That night, their third in the water, the sailors were exposed to a nerve-racking and mysterious inspection. A small boat pulled out from shore and circled the raft at 200 yards. Two Japanese trained a brace of machine guns on the Americans, but held their fire. The shivering sailors looked down the muzzles of those two machine guns until four o'clock in the morning, when a squall with six-foot waves drove the patrol craft back to the beach. After the squall passed, the PT sailors were alone again — more alone than ever, for the delirious Canterbury had swum away during the storm. Barnett, a first-rate swimmer, had chased after Canterbury to bring him back, but had lost him in the heavy seas.

That morning the five surviving sailors spied an overturned Japanese boat. It was fifteen feet long and a luxurious yacht compared to their flimsy raft, so they righted the boat and bailed it out. A crab was running about the bottom, and during the chase for this tasty tidbit the sailors let their life raft drift away. Nobody really cared; they had no fond memories of the balsa boat.

The sailors suffered horribly from thirst and they eagerly pulled in a drifting coconut, but it was dry. They were badly sunburned and covered with salt-water sores. Another chilly night and another blazing morning passed without relief.

At noon on March 10th, three Army B 25s flew over. The planes circled the frantically waving sailors, and Ensign Cutter sent a message by semaphore, a dubious method of communication with Army pilots, but better than nothing.

One bomber dropped a box which collapsed and sank. On his next pass, he dropped two more boxes and a small package fixed to a life preserver. They plunked into the sea not ten feet from the boat. The sailors eagerly tore open the packages and found food, water, cigarettes, and medicine. A marked chart showed them their position, and a message said a Catalina flying boat was on its way to pick them up.

The Catalina took its time, however, for the sailors had one more trying night to endure before the Cat, screened by two P 47s, landed on the water and picked up the five exhausted survivors.

The old problem of bad communications between

the different services bothered the PTs worse than ever in New Guinea waters.

On the morning of March 27th, Lieut. Crowell C. Hall, on Ensign George H. Guckert's PT 353, accompanied by Ensign Richard B. Secrest's 121, went into Bangula Bay to investigate a reported enemy schooner.

That morning, at Australian fighter squadron headquarters on Kiriwina Island, a careless clerk put the report of the PT patrol in the wrong file basket, so fighter pilots flew over Bangula Bay, with the information that no friendly PTs would be out. This was the same setup that had already caused repeated tragedies and near-tragedies in other waters.

At 7:45 in the morning, admittedly an unusual hour for the night-prowling PTs to be abroad, four P 40s of the Australian squadron flew over the boats. Lieut. Hall asked them, by radio, to investigate the schooner, which was beyond a dangerous reef from the PT boats. The plane pilots looked it over and told the PT skipper that it had already been badly strafed and wasn't worth attacking further.

The boats turned to go home. Four other P 40s and two Beaufighters of the same squadron came down out of the sun in a strafing run on the PTs. One of the Beaufighter pilots recognized the boats and frantically tried to call his mates off the attack, but nobody listened. The gallant Australian pilot even put his fighter between the strafing planes and the boats, trying to block the attack with his own body. No luck.

The PT officers held their men under tight discipline for several punishing runs, but the nerves of the gunners finally gave way, and each boat fired a short burst from 37- and 40-mm. cannon and the 50-caliber machine guns. The officers sharply ordered a cease-fire, and for the rest of the attack the PT crews suffered helplessly while the planes riddled their craft and killed their shipmates. Both boats exploded and sank.

The first quartet of P 40s, the planes that had chatted with Lieut. Hall, rushed back to the scene when they heard the radio traffic between the attacking fighters and suspected what was happening. They dropped a life raft to the swimming survivors and radioed headquarters the story of the disaster. Two PTs were dispatched to the rescue.

Four officers and four enlisted men were killed, four officers and eight enlisted men were wounded, two PT boats were lost to the deadly fire of the friendly fighters — all because one slipshod clerk had put a piece of paper in a wrong file basket.

Even worse was coming.

The combat zone in the Pacific was divided into

the Southwest and the South Pacific commands. Communication between the two commands at the junior officer level was almost nonexistent. Everybody was supposed to stay in his own backyard and not cross the dividing line.

On the night of April 28th, Lieut. (jg) Robert J. Williams' 347 was patrolling with Lieut. (jg) Stanley L. Manning's 350. The 347 went hard aground on a reef at Cape Pomas, only five miles from the dividing line between the south and southwest zones. Lieut. Manning passed a line to the stranded boat, and the two crews set about the all-too-familiar job of freeing a PT from an uncharted rock.

At 7 A.M. two Marine Corps Corsairs from the South Pacific zone, through faulty navigation, crossed the dividing line without knowing it. Naturally they had no word of these PTs patrolling in their area, because they weren't in their area. They attacked.

The PTs did not recognize the Corsairs as friendly, and shot one of them down. (This is an extraordinary mistake, also, for the gull-winged Corsair was probably the easiest of all warplanes on both sides to identify, especially from the head-on view presented during a strafing run.)

Three men were killed in the first attack on the 350, and both boats were badly damaged. The skippers called for help. The tender *Hilo*, at

Talasea, asked for air cover from Cape Gloucester (in the Southwest Pacific zone and hence out of communications with the South Pacific base of the Corsair pilots). The tender sent Lieut. (jg) James R. Burk to the rescue in PT 346.

The pilot of the surviving Corsair reported to his base at Green Island, in the South Pacific zone, that he had attacked two Japanese gunboats 125 feet long in Lassul Bay. (The PTs were slightly more than half that long. Lassul Bay was actually 20 miles from Cape Pomas, the true scene of the attack, and hence fifteen miles inside the South Pacific zone and not in the Southwest Pacific zone.)

Green Island scrambled four Corsairs, six Avengers, four Hellcats, and eight Dauntless dive bombers to finish off the stricken PTs. The powerful striking force, enough air-power to take on a cruiser division, found no boats in Lassul Bay, but they, too, wandered across the dividing line and found the PTs at Cape Pomas.

By then the 346 had arrived. The skipper saw the approaching planes, but recognized them as friendly types and thought they were the air cover from Cape Gloucester, so the PT crews ignored the planes and continued with the salvage and rescue work.

First hint that something had gone wrong was a shower of bombs that burst among the PT boats. The PT officers frantically tried every trick in the catalogue to identify themselves, and in despair finally turned loose their gunners, who shot down one of the planes. The loss of one of their mates angered the pilots and they pressed their attacks harder. Two of the three PTs went down.

The plane flight commander called for a Catalina rescue boat to pick up the downed pilot. The Cat never found the pilot, but instead picked up thirteen survivors of the torpedo boats. Their arrival at Green Island was the first word the horrified pilots there had that their targets had been friendly.

Three PT officers and 11 men were killed, two plane pilots were lost, four officers and nine men were wounded, two PTs and two planes were destroyed, in this useless and tragic encounter.

Most PT patrols were not as disastrous, of course, but it was a rare night that did not provide some adventure. Lieut. (jg) James Cunningham kept a diary during 1944, and a few extracts from this journal show the nature of a typical PT's blockade duty:

March 12, 1944: PTs 149 (*The Night Hawk*) and 194 patrol the north coast of New Britain. At 2300 we picked up a target on radar—

closed in and saw a small Jap surface craft. We made a run on it and found out it was aground and apparently destroyed. We destroyed it some more.

We moved to the other side of Garove Island, where we saw a craft under way heading across the mouth of the harbor. Over one part of the harbor were very high cliffs, an excellent spot for gun emplacements. We blindly chased the craft and closed in on it for a run. Just then the guns — six-inchers — opened up from the cliffs on us, and it seemed for a while that they would blow us out of the water. We left the decoy and headed out to sea, laying a smoke screen. The concussion of the exploding shells was terrific. I still believe the craft was a decoy to pull us into the harbor, and we readily took the bait. The thing that saved us was that the Japs were too eager. They fired too soon before we were really far into the harbor. On the way home, about 10 miles offshore from New Britain, we picked up three large radar pips and figured they were enemy destroyers, because they were in enemy waters and we were authorized to destroy anything in this grid sector. We chased within one mile, tracking them with radar, and got set to make our run. We could see them by eye at that range and identified them as a destroyer and two large landing craft.

We radioed for airplanes to help us with this valuable prize. Just as we started our torpedo run from about 500 yards away, the destroyer shot a recognition flare and identified themselves as friendly. It was a close call. We were within seconds of firing our fish. The task unit was off course and had wandered into a forbidden zone.

June 23, 1944: PTs 144 (*The Southern Cross*) and 189 departed Aitape Base, New Guinea, for patrol to the west.

We closed the beach at Sowam after noticing lots of lights moving. They appeared to be trucks, moving very slow. Muffled down, hidden by a black, moonless night, we sneaked to within 150 yards off the beach and waited for a truck to come around the bend and onto the short stretch of road that ran along the beach. Here came one, lights blazing. Both boats blasted away. The truck burst into flames and stopped, lights still burning. The last we saw of the truck (shore batteries fired on us immediately, so we got out) it was still standing there with headlights burning and flames leaping up in the New Guinea night. It has become quite a sport, by the way, shooting enemy trucks moving along the beach with lights on. The Japs never seem to learn. We fire at them night after night. They turn off the lights briefly, then they turn them back on again when they think we have gone. But we haven't gone. We shoot them up some more, and they turn off the lights again. And so on all night long.

The Japanese apparently smarted under these truck-busting attacks, for Lieut. Cunningham's entry three nights later tells a different story:

June 26, 1944: PTs 144 and 149 left Aitape Base, New Guinea, to patrol toward Sowam Village, where the road comes down to the beach. We were after trucks. We closed cautiously to three-quarters of a mile off the beach, then it seemed that everything opened up on us, 50 and 30 calibers, 40 mms and three-inchers. At the time they fired on us we were dead in the water, with all three engines in neutral. To get the engines into gear, the drill is to signal the engine room where the motor mack of the watch puts the engine in gear by hand. There is no way to do it from the cockpit. Then, when the gears are engaged, the skipper can control the speed by three throttles.

I was at the helm in the cockpit when the batteries opened fire, and I shoved all three throttles wide open, forgetting that the gears weren't engaged. Of course, the boat almost shook apart from the wildly racing engines, but we didn't move. The motor mack in the engine room below wrestled against me to push the throttles back. He was stronger than I was and finally got the engines slowed down enough to put them into gear. *Then* we got moving fast. We made it out to sea OK without being hit, but I sure pulled a boo boo that time.

August 28, 1944: PTs 188 and 144 west toward Hollandia, with a squad of Army radiomen aboard to contact a land patrol. This is enemy-held territory and the patrol was in hopes of taking a few prisoners.

Just after sunrise we received a radio message to pick up Jap prisoners at Ulau Mission. We proceeded to the mission and I asked some P 39s that were strafing the beach to cover us while we made the landing.

Lieut. (jg) Harry Suttenfield, skipper of the 188, and I launched a life raft and headed in to pick up prisoners from the Army patrol.

We made it OK until we got into the surf, then the breakers swamped us. There were many dead Japs lying around, and the soldiers were burning the village. The natives took the prisoners out to the boats and then swam us through the surf, pushing the raft.

We turned the prisoners over to the Army at Aitape.

More and more as the by-passed Japanese became progressively demoralized by lack of food and rest, the PTs were pressed into service as Black Marias, police vans for carrying Japanese captives from the front lines, or even from behind the lines, to Army headquarters where Intelligence officers interrogated the prisoners.

Most Japanese simply would not be captured, and killed themselves rather than surrender. Many of them made dangerous prisoners, for they surrendered only to get close enough to their captors to kill them with concealed weapons.

On the night of July 7, 1944, Lieut. (jg) William P. Hall, on the 329, dropped a fatal depth charge under a 130-foot lugger south of Cape Oransbari. The crew snagged four prisoners, one of them a lieutenant colonel, one of the highest ranking officers taken prisoner in New Guinea.

One of the prisoners attacked Lieut. Hall, who flattened him with a right to the mouth. Hall sprained his thumb and badly gashed his hand on the prisoner's teeth. He was awarded the Purple Heart for being wounded "in the face of the enemy."

Oddly enough, what few Japanese did let themselves be taken made docile, even eagerly cooperative, prisoners. PT crewmen could never tell what was coming on a Black Maria mission. Either the captives tried to kill themselves or their guards — or they tried to help the guards kill their former comrades.

On the night between March 16th and 17th, Lieut. H. M. S. Swift (the Lieut. Swift of the great air battle at Aitape) was out with Lieut. (jg) Eugene E. Klecan's 367 and 325. Off Pak Island, the two boats caught nine Japanese in a canoe. As the PTs approached, one Japanese killed himself and three others with a grenade. Another was shot by PT sailors when he resisted capture. The others came aboard willingly.

One of the captives asked for a pencil and wrote: "My name is Kamingaga. After finished Ota High School, I worked in a Yokohama army factory as an American spy. I set fire to Yokohama's arsenal. Later, I was conscripted into the Japanese army, unfortunately. I was very unhappy, but now I am very happy because I was saved by American Army. To repay your kindness I will work as a spy for your American Army."

He was turned over to skeptical Army officers, who did not make a deal with the traitorous captive.

Another Japanese canary, however, sang a most profitable song to his captors.

On the night between April 18th and 29th,

Ensign Francis L. Cappaert, in 370, and Ensign Louis A. Fanget, in 388, sank three barges in Nightingale Bay, east of Wewak.

One of the barges had been loaded with two 75-mm. cannon and 45 soldiers. The PT crews tried to pull prisoners from the water, but all but two deliberately drowned themselves.

One of the two captives said to Ensign Cappaert, "Me officer," and eagerly volunteered the advice that more barges were coming into Nightingale Bay in a few minutes. The PT skippers didn't know what kind of trap their prisoner might be baiting for them, but they stayed around anyhow. Three more barges came around the bend on schedule, however, and the PT's riddled them from ambush as "Me Officer" looked on.

The only surviving Japanese from the last three barges was a courier with a consignment of secret documents. The first lesson drilled into American sailors was that all secret documents, code books, maps, and combat instruction, were to go to the bottom if capture was imminent. The Japanese courier clung to his package, at some risk to himself, for it would have been easier to swim without it. He willingly turned over the secret papers to the PT officers.

At headquarters in Aitape, officers questioned the prisoners in their own language, and to the astonishment of the Navy, the Japanese officer dictated a barge movement timetable that helped PTs knock off fifteen barges and a picket boat in the next five nights.

Commander Robert J. Bulkley, Jr., a PT veteran who later became the official naval historian of the PT fleet (not to be confused with John Bulkeley of the MacArthur rescue mission), said of the Japanese conduct as prisoners:

"Most of them preferred death to capture, but once taken prisoner they were usually docile and willing, almost eager, to give information. And while their information might be limited, it was generally reliable. They seldom attempted deception.

"The big job was to capture them, and PT crews became fairly adept at it. One method was to crack a man over the head with a boathook and haul him up on deck. Another technique, more certain, was to drop a cargo net over the bow. Two men climbed down on the net. Other members of the crew held them by lines around their waist so that their hands were free.

"They would blackjack the floating Japanese and put a line on him so that he could be hauled aboard. Those were rough methods, but the gentle ones didn't work. The Japanese almost never took a line willingly, and as long as they were conscious would fight to free themselves from a boathook."

As a nice contrast to this careless betrayal of secret information by the Japanese, consider an American PT officer's reaction to the loss of a secret code book.

On the night of April 2nd, the 114 went aground 400 yards off Yarin, on Kairiru Island. The crew jettisoned torpedoes and depth charges and the boat was pulled off the rock by *The Southern Cross* (144). The propellers were so badly damaged, however, that the 114 was abandoned. Confidential publications, including a code book, were put into a raft, but the crew carelessly let it drift to the Japanese-held beach.

When the boats returned to the tender, the skipper reported the loss of the codes to Lieut. Commander Robert Leeson, who jumped into 129, commanded by his brother Ensign A. D. Leeson, and took off for Yarin. Ensign Edmund F. Wakelin tagged along in 134.

The two PTs hove to off the beach at Yarin, and the officers studied the situation. They could see the raft on the shore, but it was in full view of a Japanese military hut, 600 yards away, and Yarin was the site of a known powerful shore battery.

Commander Leeson wanted those books, though, and he wanted them badly, so he jumped over the side and in full daylight swam the 400 yards across the reef to the beach. While crews of the two boats watched the beach with fingers crossed, dreading the sight of the first puff of flame from the hidden shore battery, Commander Leeson pushed the raft into the water and towed it back to the boat. The secret publications were taken aboard intact.

The Japanese chose that moment — the moment just after their last chance — to wake up and plunk a salvo of shells around the boats.

Commander Leeson, not satisfied with having saved the PT code in one of the most daring exploits of the Pacific war, decided to hang around until after nightfall. After all, the PTs had come all that long way from the tender and had not yet worked any mischief.

After dark the boats slipped in close to the beach and sank two out of three heavily loaded barges. The third barge blew a 14-inch hole in the exhaust stack of the 196, knocked out the starboard engine, and started a fire.

Clarence L. Nelson, MoMM2c, put out the fire, but he and A. F. Hall, MoMM3c, passed out from the fumes. Ensign Richard Holt dropped his battle duties long enough to give the two sailors artificial respiration, and very probably saved Hall's life. The 129's engine was definitely dead, however, and nothing would bring it back to life, so Commander Leeson went on fighting with two-thirds power.

After airing out the 129's engine room, the redoubtable Leeson, with his crippled boat, led a limping charge straight into the mouth of the Japanese cannon. The two boats launched a ripple of twenty-four rockets at close range, and nothing more was heard from the beach.

When the sky turned light in the east, Commander Leeson took his sailors home.

The spearhead of the Allied advance left New Guinea for Morotai Island in September 1944. The landings there were supported by navy planes from six escort carriers. On D-Day plus one, Ensign Harold Allen Thompson took off from the deck of the carrier *Santee* in his fighter plane to strafe Japanese positions around Wasile Bay on nearby Halmahera. His sortie touched off one of the most heroic adventures of the Pacific war.

According to the report of the carrier division commander: "Success of the landings on Morotai depended upon keeping the Japanese continually on the defensive . . . thus making it impossible for them to launch counteroffensives until American forces were established in strength on the smaller island [Morotai]."

Ensign Thompson's job was to beat up Japanese barges in Wasile Bay. While he was in a steep dive on his fourth strafing run, the Japanese made a direct hit with a heavy shell on Ensign Thompson's plane.

The carrier division commander reports:

"The next thing he knows he was being blown *upward* with such force that his emergency gear was even blown out of his pockets. He pulled the ripcord and on the way down he found himself literally looking down the barrels of almost every gun in the Japanese positions about 300 yards away.

"On hitting the water, he discovered that his left hand had been badly torn, presumably by shrapnel. His life jacket had been torn in front and would only half inflate. His main idea was to get away from the beach and out into the bay, but progress was difficult."

His comrades stayed with the downed pilot and strafed the beach until a PBY patrol plane came, but the rescue Cat could not land. The pilot dropped a life raft instead, and Ensign Thompson climbed aboard. He put a tourniquet on his bleeding hand and then paddled to a pier to hide in the shelter of a camouflaged lugger.

"These pilots heroically covered all the beach area with a devastating attack so that little or no fire could be directed at the pilot in the raft," says the division report. "The attacks drove the Japanese gunners to shelter, but after the attacks they returned to their guns."

Ensign Thompson said it was a wonderful show to watch, but it was a tragically expensive show. Ensign William P. Bannister was hit and crashed 150 yards from Ensign Thompson, gallantly giving his life to save his fellow pilot.

Ensign Paul W. Lindskog was also hit, but flew his wobbly plane safely to a crash landing outside the Japanese lines. Almost all the planes were holed, but they continued the strafing runs until Thompson had worked his way behind the armored lugger.

When fuel ran low, another flight of fighters came up to strafe, and the carrier set up a system of shuttle flights to keep the beach under constant attack.

So far, so good. But how to get Ensign Thompson out of Wasile Bay if a Catalina couldn't land there? After all, the fighters couldn't cover the wounded pilot till the war was over. Somebody thought about the PT fleet, and so the carrier division commander called the PT tender *Oyster Bay* and asked if there was anything the PTs could do.

Certainly there was something the PTs could do; they could rescue the pilot.

Lieut. Arthur Murray Preston, commander of Squadron Thirty-Three, picked two all-volunteer crews, and they put to sea in Lieut. Wilfred Tatro's 489 and Lieut. (jg) Hershel F. Boyd's 363.

The boat arrived off the mouth of Wasile Bay in the middle of the afternoon. Lieut. Preston knew there was a minefield, backed up by a light shore battery, at the eastern side of the entrance. A powerful and hitherto unsuspected battery opened fire on the western shore, however, and Preston chose the lesser danger of the minefield and the lighter battery.

Shorefire from both beaches was so heavy that the PTs had to fall back. The fighter pilots spotted their difficulty and made strafing runs on the shore batteries. The Japanese guns still fired on the PTs, but at a slower rate, and Lieut. Preston decided to risk a run through the narrow straits.

"Strafing by the planes unquestionably reduced the rate of fire to make a safe passage through the straits possible," said Lieut. Preston. "Safe" passage, indeed!

The inside was no improvement on the entrance, for the bay was small and ringed with guns, all of which could reach the PTs. The shooting was steadily improving also as Japanese gunners found the range.

Lieut. (jg) George O. Stouffer called from his torpedo bomber to ask Lieut. Preston if he would like to have a little smoke between the PTs and the shore gunners.

Would he like a little smoke? Just all there is.

Stouffer flew between the PTs and the beach,

laying a dense curtain of smoke to blind the gunners. He dropped one smoke pot squarely over a particularly dangerous gun battery, blanking off its view in all directions. The plane also dropped a smoke float to mark the location of the downed pilot's raft.

During the approach of the two PTs to the armored lugger, they added their guns to those of the planes lashing the beach, but lookouts kept a nervous watch on the Japanese boat — nobody could be sure that the lugger was not manned by enemy sailors waiting to shoot up the rescue craft at the moment they were most occupied with the downed pilot. The closer the boats came to the lugger, the more the planes concentrated their fire on the nearby beach.

"This strafing was maintained at an almost unbelievable intensity during the entire time the boats were in the vicinity of the downed pilot. This was the ultimate factor in the success of the mission," reads Lieut. Preston's report, which makes no mention of another factor — the incredible tenaciousness of the two PT crews.

The first smoke screen was beginning to thin dangerously when the 363 hove to beyond the lugger and raked the beach with its guns.

The 489 went alongside the lugger.

"Immediately and on their own initiative, Lieut. D. F. Seaman and C. D. Day, MoMM1c, dove overboard and towed the pilot in his boat to the stern of 489. The pilot was in no condition to do this for himself and appeared to be only partly conscious of his circumstances and surroundings," wrote Preston. The rescue took ten minutes.

The PTs were not through fighting yet. Lieut. Preston remembered that the primary mission of PTs in those waters was destruction of Japanese coastal shipping, so he ordered the two PTs to put a few holes in the lugger and set it afire before leaving.

The fighter cover ran low on fuel, and there was a near-disastrous breakdown in the shuttle timetable.

Preston reports what happened:

"While we were hove-to picking up Thompson there was a group of planes giving us the closest possible cover and support. As we left the scene the planes did not remain quite as close to us as they had previously. . . . It was shortly after this that we learned that the fighters were critically low on fuel and some of them out of ammunition. Nevertheless, they were still answering our calls to quiet one gun or another, sometimes having to dive on the gun positions without firing, because their own magazines were empty. . . . They were magnificent."

The PTs zigzagged across the minefield with heavy shells bursting within ten yards on all sides.

When they finally broke into the open sea and roared away from the enemy beach, Ensign Thompson had been in the water for seven hours, the PTs had been under continuous close-range fire from weapons of all calibers for two and one-half hours. The boats were peppered with shrapnel, but, miraculously, none of the PT sailors had been scratched.

Dr. Eben Stoddard had a job, though, trying to save the pilot's left hand, which was so badly mangled by shrapnel that three fingers dangled loosely.

The seven hours of protective strafing had blown up an ammunition dump, destroyed a fuel dump, wrecked stores, silenced four heavy gun positions at least temporarily, and certainly prevented the Japanese from getting to the downed pilot.

Lieut. Preston was awarded the Congressional Medal of Honor for this action, one of the two Congressional Medals of Honor awarded to PT sailors. (The other was given to Lieut. John Bulkeley for his exploits during the fall of the Philippines.) The two swimmers and the two skippers won the Navy Cross. Every other member of the two crews won a Silver Star.

Ironically, the day after incredible escape of all PT hands without injury, Lieut. Tatro, skipper of the 489, while working on a 20-mm gun, let a wrench slip and a trunnion spring threw the heavy tool into his forehead, injuring him seriously.

By November 1944, there was no more work for the PTs in New Guinea, and the last patrol was made just twenty-three months after the first one, 1,500 miles to the east. The PT navy in New Guinea had grown from one small tender and six boats to eight tenders and 14 squadrons.

Almost nightly action had taken a terrible toll of the Japanese. The shore was littered with the wreckage of *daihatsus* and the jungle was littered with the skeletons of thousands of Japanese soldiers who had died for lack of supplies.

Major General F. H. Berryman, Commander of the Second Australian Corps, wrote the PT commander:

> The following evidence emerging from the recent operations will illustrate the cumulative effect of the activities of your command:
>
> A. The small degree to which the enemy has used artillery indicates a shortage of ammunition.
>
> B. The enemy, in an endeavor to protect his barges, has been forced to dispose his normal field artillery over miles of coast when those guns might well have been used in the coastal sector against our land troops.
>
> C. Many Japanese diary entries describe the

shortage of rations and the regular fatigues of foraging parties to collect native food, which is beginning to be increasingly difficult to obtain.

D. A Japanese prisoner of war stated that three days' rice, augmented by native food, now has to last nine days. This is supported by the absence of food and the presence of native roots on enemy dead.

E. There is definite evidence that the enemy has slaughtered and eaten his pack-carrying animals.

From the above you will see how effective has been the work of your squadrons and how it has contributed to the recent defeat of the enemy.

The war in New Guinea was over, but the Allies were still a long way from Tokyo. Across the water were the Philippine Islands, garrisoned with tens of thousands of Japanese. There was hard fighting ahead for the PTs.

6.

The War in Europe:

Mediterranean

WHILE AMERICANS and their Allies were fighting the Japanese in the Pacific, on the other side of the world their comrades in arms grappled in a Titanic struggle with the other two Axis powers. Half of the European Axis partnership was halfhearted Italy, but the other half was the martial and determined state of Germany, led by an insane genius at the black arts of killing named Hitler.

The naval war in the coastal waters of Europe was eminently suitable to torpedo-boat operations. The British had been making spectacular use of motor torpedo boats for years — in fact, American PTs had been patterned after British models. The Axis powers also used torpedo boats. German E-boats prowled the English Channel and the Mediterranean. Even the Italian MAS boats made Allied Mediterranean naval commanders nervous, for the torpedo boat had been an Italian specialty since its invention and the officers who manned Italian small craft were the most aggressive and warlike in all the Italian Armed Forces.

American troops went ashore in Northwest Africa on November 8, 1942. (On the other side of the world, the Japanese were just forming the massive relief fleet that was smashed and dispersed definitively a week later in the great three-day sea battle of Guadalcanal.) The United States Navy rushed to put American torpedo boats into the Mediterranean to join the British in harrying Axis shipping.

In New Orleans, in late 1942, Squadron Fifteen was organized. Its commander was Lieut. Commander Stanley Barnes, destined to become probably the most dashing of all American PT sailors, as the squadron itself was to become the most spectacularly successful PT command in either theatre.

On commissioning day the squadron members didn't feel elated about their future. Their first assignment was to patrol the warm blue waters off Midway Island, far behind the fighting lines in the Pacific. While the Tulagi PTs fought almost nightly battles with Tanaka's Tokyo Express, Squadron Fifteen was promised long, lazy afternoons of cribbage, 3,500 miles behind the combat zone. Its assignment gave its members slight headaches every time they thought about it.

Lieut. Commander Barnes assured his squadron mates that somehow, somewhere, he was going to find somebody for them to fight. But nobody believed him — not even he, as he later confessed.

The squadron sailed for the Panama Canal and was well on the way to the gentle duties of Midway when the radioman came running with a dispatch.

Orders to Midway were canceled! "Report to Commander in Chief, Atlantic Fleet, in Norfolk," the message read.

At the giant Virginia naval base, Barnes had his conference with the upper echelons of brass and rushed back to his squadron mates with the news that they were indeed going to find somebody somewhere to fight. They were going to the Mediterranean as the first American torpedo-boat squadron on the European scene.

The barman at the Navy Officers' Club in Norfolk was famous in those days — and may still be — for his Stingers, a most appropriate toast to duty in the Mediterranean mosquito fleet.

The 201 and 204 crossed the Atlantic immediately as deck passengers on the S. S. *Enoree,* and Lieut. Commander Barnes followed on the S. S. *Housatonic,* with 205 and 208. The *Enoree* arrived at Gibraltar first, on April 13th. Boats were in the water the next day, and Lieut. Edwin A. Dubose — also destined to make a name as a brilliant PT sailor — took them to the British torpedo-boat dock, loaded a full cargo of torpedoes, and set sail for Oran in North Africa. Skippers of the other boats followed as fast as longshoremen could swing the PTs into the water.

Disappointment awaited the crews in Oran, where the high command sent the boats to Cherchel, 300 miles from the nearest action, for an indefinite period of training.

"I decided to take the bull by the horns and bum a ride to Algiers in an Army truck to see Vice Admiral Henry K. Hewitt," said Lieut. Commander Barnes.

Admiral Hewitt was commander of all U. S. Naval forces in northwest African waters, and Barnes hoped to persuade him that the PTs should be based at Bône, 265 miles farther east and within easy reach of trouble at the front.

"That trip took me several hours and by the time I got there I was chagrined to find that orders had already been issued and Lieut. Richard H. O'Brien, my next in command, had gotten the boats under way and was in Algiers before me. The admiral himself brought me up to date with the information that my boats were already there. Most embarrassing!"

The next day, April 27th, Lieut. Dubose took his boats to the forward base at Bône, and that night they went out on their first patrol in combat waters.

Bône was also the British forward base for motor torpedo boats and gunboats. Like the American PTs, the British MTBs carried torpedoes, but the British had already converted some patrol craft to gunboats, similar to the heavily gunned PTs of New Guinea. The gunboats carried no torpedoes.

The British had been fighting in the Mediterranean for months, so American PTs made most of their early patrols with British officers aboard to tip them off to local conditions.

The North African campaign was drawing to a close. General Erwin Rommel's crack Afrika Korps was bottled up in Tunisia, and torpedo boats patrolled nightly to prevent escape of Rommel's soldiers to Sicily, just 90 miles across the strait from Tunisia's Cape Bon.

Lieut. Commander Barnes, in the 106, joined three British torpedo boats under Lieut. Dennis Germaine, in a patrol down the east side of Cape Bon. At Ras Idda Bay, Lieut. Germaine took one British MTB inside the harbor to investigate a possible target.

Lieut. Commander Barnes continues the story:

"Pretty soon Germaine came up on the radio with the startling statement that there are lots of ships in there, so I took the remaining British boats with me and started in. It was as black as the inside of your pocket, but sure enough, right there in front of me was a ship.

"By the time we saw it against the dark background of the land we were inside the torpedo-aiming range and had to go all the way around the other side of it before getting a good shot.

"Thinking there were other targets around, I lined up and fired only one torpedo — our first!

"It ran hot and straight, and after what seemed like an interminable time made a beautiful hit forward. The whole ship blew up in our faces, scattering pieces of debris all around us and on deck. Just like the movies.

"We immediately started to look for other ships but could find none. Neither could we find our British friend, who, it turned out, was temporarily aground, so we just eased around trying to rendezvous. Pretty soon he found us — and promptly fired two fish at us, one of which passed right under our bow and the other under the stern, much to our alarm and his subsequent embarrassment.

"About half an hour later, bombers started working over the airfield a couple of miles away, and with the light of the flares we managed to join up with Germaine.

"I personally think that ship was aground — the ship we torpedoed — although it certainly made a fine spectacle going up, and one of our officers who was along that night subsequently flew over the area in a plane and reported it sitting nicely on the bottom.

"Actually, Germaine had not seen any ships and

had mistaken some peculiar rock formations for a group of enemy vessels."

That was not the last mistake of the British Navy. Unused to working with their new Allies, the British boats took one more near-lethal crack at American PTs.

Lieut. Dubose, in Lieut. (jg) Eugene S. Clifford's 212, with Lieut. Richard H. O'Brien in 205, left Bône on the night of May 10th to patrol Cape Bon. On the way home after a dull night, the two boats cut deep into the Gulf of Tunis to keep clear of a British destroyer area.

The Gulf of Tunis was supposed to belong to torpedo boats that night, but two British destroyers came roaring out of the night on an opposite course only 900 yards away. The destroyers opened up with machine guns as they passed, so the PTs fired two emergency recognition starshells and ran away behind a smoke screen.

Two German E-boats, lurking in the darkness for a crack at the two destroyers, opened up on the PTs instead, and the British took *all* the torpedo boats under fire, distributing shells and bullets on American and German boats with impartiality.

The two PT skippers were given the thorny tactical problem of dodging friendly destroyer fire while simultaneously taking on the German boats. Lieut. Clifford turned back through his own smoke, surprised the E-boats at close range when he burst out of the screen, and raked the enemy with his machine-gun batteries. He ran back into the smoke before they could swing their mounts to bear on him, so he couldn't report results of his attack, but destroyer sailors saw one of the E-boats burst into flame. The other ran from the fight.

Not so the destroyers. They chased the PTs for an hour, firing starshells and salvos from their main battery. Fortunately their shooting was poor, and the PTs got out of the battle with only a few machine-gun holes.

Days later one of the destroyer skippers called to apologize. "We hadn't been able to find any action in our assigned patrol area," he said, "so we decided to have a bit of a look in the PT area."

The destroyer skipper's action was dashing and bold, but it was also a fine way to catch a friendly torpedo in his own ship or to kill a dozen or so of his Allies.

Three E-boats had attacked the destroyers at the precise instant that the American PTs arrived on the scene, according to the British officer who had heard a German radio discussion of a plan to attack the destroyers. Naturally the alarmed British began blasting at any torpedo boat in sight. Everybody saw Dubose's recognition flares, but took them for tracer fire, a common mistake.

A strange aftermath of the running gun battle was

the naval occupation of the great port of Bizerte by a lone PT.

The 205 lost the other boat in the night and put into Bizerte for gasoline. The port had just been taken by Allied troops a few hours earlier.

The shore batteries, now in friendly hands, nevertheless fired the "customary few rounds" at the arriving PT boat, but the imperturbable Lieut. O'Brien said: "The shots were wide, so I continued in and tied up at the dock."

Two hours later a newsreel photographer asked O'Brien to move his PT out of the way so he could photograph some British landing ships just arriving as "the first Allied craft to enter Bizerte."

Lieut. O'Brien wondered what his own boat was if not an Allied craft, and he had been in Bizerte long enough to be bored with the place, but he patiently moved aside.

The brush-off from the newsreel man was only the beginning of the stepchild treatment the PTs suffered at Bizerte.

Squadron Fifteen cleaned up a hangar and scrounged spare parts and machinery from all over the city. When the big boys came into the harbor, their skippers were delighted with the tidy PT base and ruthlessly pushed the little boys out the door.

"We cleaned up half the buildings in Bizerte," said one veteran of Squadron Fifteen. "As fast as we made a place presentable, we were kicked out. We ended up with only a fraction of our original space, and we had to fight tooth and nail for that."

Late in May the squadron was filled out to full strength and the newly arrived boats were fitted with radar. The British boats did not have it, so the two torpedo-boat fleets began to experiment with a system of radio signals to vector British boats to American radar targets in coordinated simultaneous attacks.

After the collapse of the Afrika Korps in Tunisia in mid-May 1943, all of North Africa was in Allied hands and Allied attention turned toward Europe, across the narrow sea.

To mislead the enemy about the spot chosen by the Allies for the next landing, British secret agents of the Royal Navy elaborated a fantastic hoax worthy of the cheapest dime novel. The amazing thing is that it worked.

The British dressed the corpse of a man who had died of pneumonia in the uniform of a major in the Royal Marines. They stuffed his pockets with forged credentials as a Major William Martin, and they planted forged letters on the body to make him look like a courier between the highest Allied commands. The letters "revealed" that the Allies would next land in Sardinia and Greece. The body was pushed overboard from a submarine off the coast of Spain. It washed up on the beach as an apparent victim of a plane crash and was frisked by an Axis agent, just as the British had hoped.

Hitler was taken in by the hoax and gave priority to reinforcing Sardinia and Greece, widely separated, not only from each other, but also from Sicily, where the Allies were actually going to land.

To help along the confusion of Axis officers (most of whom were of a less romantic nature than their *Fuehrer* and were not taken in by the Major William Martin fraud), the Allies mounted another hoax almost as childishly imaginative as the planted cadaver trick.

On D-Day, July 10, 1943, Commander Hunter R. Robinson in PT 213 led a flotilla of ten Air Force crash boats to Cape Granitola, at the far western tip of Sicily, as far as it could get from the true landing beaches around both sides of the southeastern horn of the triangular island.

The crash boats and the PT were supposed to charge about offshore during the early hours of D-Day, sending out phony radio messages, firing rockets, playing phonograph records of rattling anchor chains and the clanking and chuffing of landing-craft engines. The demonstration didn't seem to fool anybody ashore, but the little craft tried.

Most of Squadron Fifteen was busy elsewhere on the morning of D-Day and narrowly missed being butchered in one of those ghastly attacks from friendly forces that were so dangerous to PT boats.

One force of American soldiers was going ashore at Licata. Twenty-four miles west, at Port Empedocle, was a flotilla of Italian torpedo boats which so worried the high command that Empedocle had been ruled out as a possible landing beach. To keep the Italian boats off the back of the main naval force, a special screen was thrown between Port Empedocle and the transport fleet, a screen of seventeen of Lieut. Commander Barnes' PTs and the destroyer *Ordronaux*. After the war, historians discovered that the much-feared Italian torpedo boats at Empedocle had accidentally bumped into the invasion fleet the night before the landings, and had fled in panic to a new base at Trapani at the farthest western tip of the island.

Another one of those terrible blind battles between friendly forces was prepared when nobody told the westernmost destroyers of the main landing force that PTs would be operating nearby. The skippers of the destroyers *Swanson* and *Roe*, nervous anyway because of the Italian torpedo-boat nest at Empedocle, charged into the PT patrol area when they saw radar pips on their screens. Lieut. Commander Barnes flashed a recognition signal, but the destroyer signal crews ignored it.

Just as the destroyer unit commander was about to open fire at 1,500 yards, *Roe* rammed *Swanson* at the forward stack. *Roe*'s bow folded up and

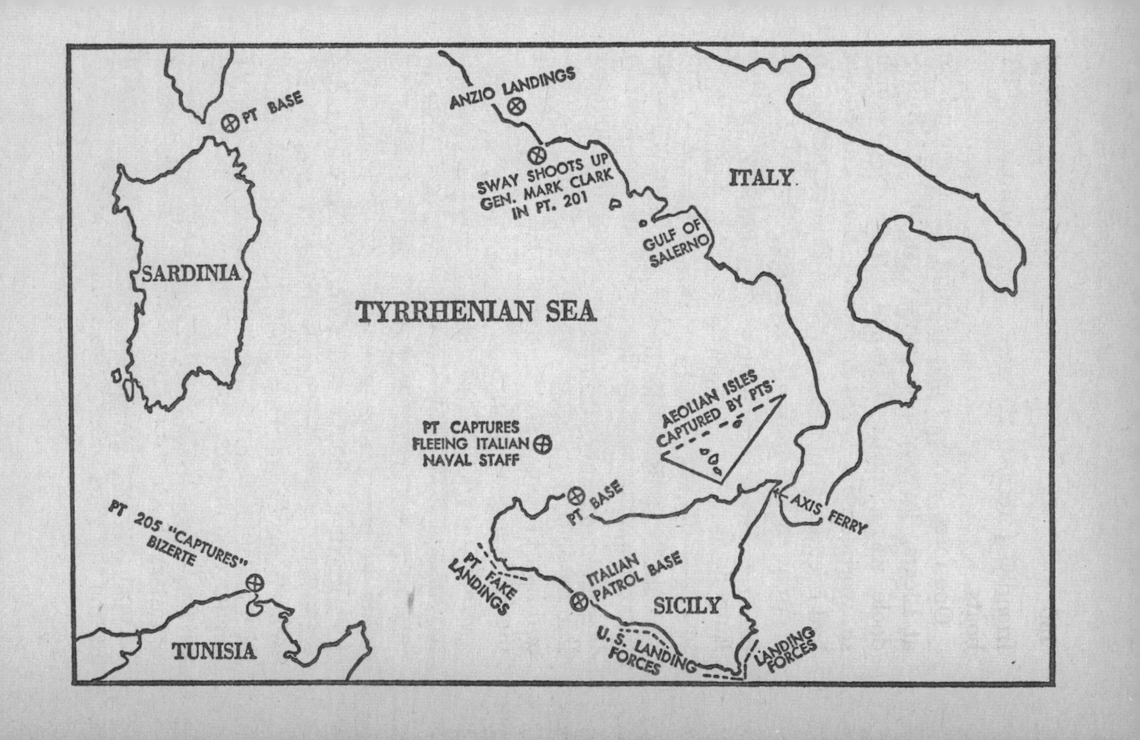
PT BASE
ANZIO LANDINGS
SWAY SHOOTS UP
GEN. MARK CLARK
IN PT. 201
ITALY
GULF OF
SALERNO
SARDINIA
TYRRHENIAN SEA
PT CAPTURES
FLEEING ITALIAN
NAVAL STAFF
AEOLIAN ISLES
CAPTURED BY PTS
PT BASE
AXIS FERRY
PT 205 "CAPTURES"
BIZERTE
PT FAKE
LANDINGS
ITALIAN
PATROL BASE
SICILY
TUNISIA
U. S. LANDING
FORCES
LANDING
FORCES

both ships went dead in the water. The *Swanson's* forward fireroom was partly flooded. Both ships had to be sent to the rear for repairs, carrying with them, of course, their five-inch cannon which were sorely missed by the assault troops of that morning's landings.

Two nights later, on July 12th, Lieut. Commander Barnes split his PTs into two forces to escort twelve crash boats for another fraudulent demonstration of strength at Cape Granitola. The two forces ran parallel to the beach behind smoke, and noisily imitated the din of a force a thousand times their true size.

Searchlights blazed out from the shore, and the second salvo from shore batteries landed so close to the boats that the skippers hauled out to sea.

"The shore batteries were completely alerted," said Lieut. Commander Barnes. "Apparently the enemy was convinced that a landing was about to take place when it detected the 'large number' of boats in our group approaching the beach, for they opened a heavy and accurate fire with radar control. . . . I immediately reversed course and opened the range. One shell damaged the rudder of a crash boat and another fell ten yards astern of a PT.

"The demonstration was called a success and we withdrew."

The next day enemy newspapers reported that

an attempted landing on the southwest coast of Sicily had been bloodily repulsed.

Soldiers of the American and British landing forces swarmed over Sicily, taking Italian prisoners by the hundreds. Some Americans were amused, some depressed by the standard joke of many surrendering Italian soldiers: "Don't be sorry for me. I'm going to America and you're staying in Sicily."

Palermo, major city on the northwestern coast, fell to the Allies on July 22nd, and the jaunty boats of Squadron Fifteen were the first Allied naval power to show the flag in the harbor. They picked their way through the sunken hulks of fifty ships. The dockside was a shambles. In a word, Palermo was a typical PT advanced base.

The squadron moved up from Bizerte the same day and began patrolling the Tyrrhenian Sea, those waters boxed in by Sicily, Italy, Sardinia and Corsica.

Isolated in the Tyrrhenian Sea, about thirty miles north of Palermo, is the island of Ustica. On the first Tyrrhenian patrol Lieut. Commander Barnes led his boats toward Ustica to see what was going on in those backwaters of the war.

"At dawn we were off Ustica," the squadron leader reports. "First thing, we saw a fishing boat putt-putting toward Italy. We found a handful of very scared individuals crawling out from under the floor plates, hopefully waving white handkerchiefs. This was the staff of an Italian admiral at Trapani [site of the Italian torpedo-boat base at the western tip of Sicily, bypassed by the fall of Palermo].

"Only reason we didn't get the admiral was that he was late getting down to the dock and his staff said the hell with him.

"In addition to a few souvenir pistols and binoculars, we captured a whole fruit crate of thousand-lira notes which we reluctantly turned over to Army authorities later. One of the other boats saw a raft with seven Germans on it, feebly paddling out to sea. We picked them up too."

The next night three PTs of Squadron Fifteen patrolled to the Strait of Messina, right against the toe of the Italian mainland itself, and two nights later, off Cape Vaticano, the same three boats – under Lieut. E. A. Arbuckle – found the 8,800-ton Italian freighter *Viminale* being towed toward Naples by a tug.

For some reason, the freighter was being towed backward, almost causing the PT skippers to take a lead in the wrong direction, but they sank both ships in the first U.S. Naval victory in the Tyrrhenian Sea.

On the night of July 26th, near the island of Stromboli, three PTs commanded by Lieut. J. B.

Mutty ran into their first F-lighters, those powerfully armed German landing craft and general-duty blockade runners that were to become the Number One enemy of PTs in the Mediterranean.

The F-lighters were slow and cumbersome, but they were armored and mounted extremely heavy antiaircraft batteries which could saw a PT into toothpicks. Gun turrets were lined with cement and often mounted the much-feared 88-mm. rifle, thus enormously outgunning the PTs.

Holds of the F-lighters were so well compartmented that they could take terrible punishment without going down. With only four and one-half feet of draft, they usually slid over PT torpedoes, set to run at eight-foot depth. An F-lighter was a serious opponent for a destroyer and much more than a match for a PT— in theory.

The three PT skippers at Stromboli didn't know about that theory, however, and probably wouldn't have hesitated about attacking even if they had known how dangerous an F-lighter was. They fired six fish and thought they had blown up two of the F-lighters, but postwar assessment says No. Neither side was badly hurt in this first duel, but more serious fighting was to come.

The next night, July 28th, three boats commanded by Lieut. Arbuckle fired at what the skippers thought were F-lighters, but were really Italian torpedo boats. American torpedoes passed harmlessly under the hulls of the enemy boats;

Italian machine-gunners punched sixty holes in PT 218 and seriously wounded three officers, including Lieut. Arbuckle. The boat got back to Palermo with 18 inches of water sloshing about below decks.

The F-lighters were ferrying Axis troops out of Sicily, across the Strait of Messina. The Allied high command had hoped to catch the whole Axis force on Sicily in a gigantic trap, and the Messina ferry had to be broken up.

The Navy tried a combined torpedo boat-destroyer operation against the ferry, but as usual, communications between the American ships were bad and the destroyers opened fire on their own PTs.

The first salvo from the American destroyers splashed water on the PT decks. The PTs were five knots slower than the American cans. (Remember those news stories, in the early days of the war, about the dazzling 70-knot PTs — fast enough to "run rings around any warship afloat"? During the summer of 1943, few of the Squadron Fifteen boats could top 25 to 27 knots.) Because they couldn't run away from their deadly friends and because they feared American gunnery more than they feared Italian gunnery, the PT boats actually ran for the enemy shore to snuggle under the protection of Italian batteries on Cape Rasocolmo. The enemy guns obligingly fired on the American destroyers and drove them away. The PT sailors went home, enormously grateful to the enemy for his involuntary but effective act of good will.

In August the Axis powers ferried most of their power to the mainland across the three-mile-wide Strait of Messina, in a brilliant escape from the Sicilian trap.

PT skippers knew about the evacuation, but had orders to stay away from the scene. British torpedo boats that tried to break up the evacuation train were badly mauled by shore batteries. One torpedo boat disappeared, with all hands, in the flash of a direct hit from a gigantic nine and one-half-inch shell.

Chafing at the order that kept it out of the action, the PT command dreamed up an operation to relieve the tedium. It decided to mount an invasion of its own to capture an island.

Setting up a jury-rig invasion staff, the officers pored over charts, looking for the ideal enemy island to add to the PT bag. Lieut. Dubose, returning from a fight with German mine sweepers on the night of August 15th, picked up an Italian merchant seaman from a small boat off Lipari Island, in the Aeolian Group, a few miles northwest of the Strait of Messina. The sailor said there were no Germans on Lipari and the islanders would undoubtedly be delighted to be captured by the American Navy.

When the admiral heard the squadron's proposal he radioed: "Demand the unconditional surrender of the islands, suppress any opposition, bring back as prisoners all who are out of sympathy."

Three PTs, their crews beefed up by 17 extra sailors, six soldiers and a military government man – with a destroyer following behind as main fire support – sailed into Lipari Harbor at 11 A.M. on August 17th, guns manned and trained on the beach. At precisely the critical moment, the destroyer hove into view around a headland, giving the impression of a mighty fleet backing up the puny invaders.

The commandant of the Italian naval garrison came down to the dock himself to handle mooring lines for his captors.

The American Military Government man stepped gracefully ashore in the first assault wave and set up a government on the spot. PT men rounded up military prisoners, hauled down the Italian and hoisted the American flag.

The Italian commodore slipped off in the excitement and tried to burn his papers, but a sailor persuaded him to stop by pressing the muzzle of a 45 automatic to his brow.

Sailors confiscated the documents and collected souvenirs, while the commandant radioed the other islands in the group and the PT skippers accepted their surrender by long distance. Only Stromboli resisted, so the PTs chugged over to find out what was holding up the breaking out of peace on that volcanic pimple.

They found an Italian chief petty officer and a 30-man detail, blowing up their radio equipment. The American sailors indignantly halted the sabotage — then destroyed the stuff themselves.

All the Italian navy saboteurs were put under armed guard for transport to American prisons in Sicily, but a pregnant woman burst into sobs, pleading that one of the men was her husband, a fisherman who had never spent a night away from Stromboli in his life. Six other women joined their wails to the chorus. The local priest assured Lieut. Dubose that their stories were true, so Dubose granted the prisoners a reprieve.

The boats returned to Lipari, picked up fifty merry military prisoners there, and departed for Palermo to the cheers of the entire town.

Messina fell that same day, and the Sicilian campaign was over.

Three weeks after the fall of Sicily, on the morning of September 9th, Allied troops went ashore in force on the mainland around the magnificent Bay of Salerno, just across a headland from Naples, second port of Italy.

Invasion chores were not strenuous for the PTs — a little anti-E-boat patrol in the bay and some light courier and taxi service for Army and Navy brass. Dull duty, but the boats had to fly low and slow, because they were almost out of aviation gasoline; their tanker had failed to arrive on schedule.

By October 4th, however, the gasoline was in and the British had taken a splendid harbor at La Maddalena, off northeast Sardinia, so Squadron Fifteen sailed to Sardinia, from where it and the British boats could prey on enemy traffic north of Naples. Almost immediately, part of Squadron Fifteen moved still farther north to Bastia, on Corsica, which the Free French had just taken back from the enemy. These two bases put PTs on the flanks of coastal shipping lanes deep in the heart of enemy waters. Genoa itself, the largest port in Italy, was now within reach of the squadron's torpedoes. Hunting was especially good in the Tuscan Archipelago, a group of islets and rocks between the PT base and the mainland.

Something had to be done about the PT torpedoes, however, for the squadron was equipped with old Mark VIIIs, built in the 1920's, crotchety, unreliable, and worst of all, designed to run so far below the surface that they couldn't touch a shallow-draft F-lighter.

PT torpedomen tinkered with their fish to set them for a shallow run, but the Mark VIII was frisky without eight feet of water to hold it down. The shallow-set Mark VIIIs porpoised, alternately leaping from the water and diving like sportive dolphins. PT skippers set them shallow anyhow, and fired them with the idea that there was a fifty-fifty chance the porpoising torpedo would be on the upswing when it got to the target and might at least punch a hole in the side.

In Italy, as the contending armies fought slowly up the peninsula, the German situation became somewhat like the Japanese situation at that same moment in New Guinea. Powerful Allied air strikes disrupted supply by rail from Genoa and Rome to the front, so the Germans had to rely on waterborne transport to run down the coast at night.

To protect themselves from marauding Allied destroyers, the Germans fenced off a channel close to the shore with a barrier of thousands of underwater mines. At salient points they mounted heavy, radar-directed cannon – some as big as nine and one-half inches in bore – to keep raiding destroyers pushed away from the mine-protected channel.

The mine fields worked. Deep-draft destroyers did not dare chase Axis vessels too close to the beach. The shallow-bottom PTs skimmed over the top of the mine fields, however, so the Germans countered by arming many types of small ships as anti-PT boats. They took over a type of Italian warship called a torpedo boat, but actually a small destroyer, fast and heavily gunned, eminently qualified for PT-elimination work.

Night patrols became lively, with PTs harrying

Axis coastal shipping and the Germans hunting them with E-boats and armed minesweepers, torpedo boats and F-lighters.

The first brawl after the PTs set up base on Sardinia and Corsica came on the night between October 22nd and 23rd. Three PTs, under the indefatigable Lieut. Dubose, sneaked up on a cargo ship escorted by four E-boats and minesweepers. The PTs fired a silent spread of four, and the cargo ship disappeared in a violent blast. Lieut. (jg) T. L. Sinclair was lining up his 212 to work a little more destruction, when a wobbly out-of-control Mark VIII torpedo from another PT flashed by under his stern.

"How many have you fired?" Lieut. Dubose asked Lieut. Sinclair by radio.

"None yet. I'm too damned busy dodging yours."

Between Giglio and Elba, in the Tuscan Archipelago, on the night between November 2nd and 3rd, two PTs, under Lieut. Richard H. O'Brien, made a torpedo run on a subchaser and blew a satisfactorily fatal hole in the hull with a solid hit. The stricken vessel went down, all right, but it went down fighting, and one of the last incendiary bullets from the dying ship bored through the gasoline tank of the 207, touching off an explosion that blew off a deck hatch. Flames as high as the radar mast shot through the open hatchway.

A radioman turned on a fire extinguisher, threw

it into the flaming compartment, and slammed down the hatch again. Miraculously, the fire went out.

Early in November, Lieut. Commander Barnes, who had been doing some deep thinking about the war against F-lighters, came up with a new tactical idea.

His reasoning was: PTs are radar-equipped, hence better than British boats at finding enemy vessels and maneuvering for attack; British torpedo boats use better torpedoes than American Mark VIIIs, for they are faster and carry heavier explosive charges; British gunboats have heavier firepower than PTs, for they usually carry at least six-pounder cannon and so can take on heavier opponents.

So Lieut. Commander Barnes and his British counterpart worked out a scheme of joint patrolling, the Americans acting as a scout force and finding targets by radar. The targets once found, the PTs were to guide the British boats in a coordinated attack. From November 1943 until April 1944, joint patrols had fourteen actions, in which skippers claimed 15 F-lighters, two E-boats, a tug and an oil barge sunk; three F-lighters, a destroyer, a trawler, and an E-boat damaged.

As winter came on, winds mounted and seas ran high, but the PTs maintained their patrols. On the foul night of November 29th, Lieut. (jg) Eugene A.

Clifford took his 204 out with another PT for a patrol near Genoa. Within two hours the wind built up to 35 knots, water smashed over the bow in blinding sheets and drowned out the radar, visibility dropped to less than a hundred yards. The PTs gave up the patrol and turned back toward Bastia. In the stormy night the boats were separated and the 204 plugged along alone, lookouts almost blinded by the spray.

Out of the darkness four E-boats appeared within slingshot range, laboring on an opposite course. A fifth E-boat "crossed the T," but not fast enough, for the PT and the E-boat struck each other a glancing blow with their bows.

From a ten-yard range, the two small craft ripped into each other with every gun that would bear. The other four E-boats joined the affray, and for fifteen seconds the 204 was battered from broad-jumping distance by the concentrated fire of five enemy boats.

The PT escaped in the darkness and the crew set about counting its wounds. Bullets had torn up torpedo tubes, ventilators, ammunition lockers, gun mounts. The deck and the superstructure were a ruin of splinters. The engine room had a hundred new and undesired ventilation apertures.

The skipper polled his crew to prepare the melancholy roll of dead and wounded. Not a man had been nicked! The gas tank was intact. The engines still purred along like electric clocks. The

204, outnumbered five to one, had stood up to a fifteen-second eyeball-to-eyeball Donnybrook and was nevertheless bringing all its sailors home in good health.

Two of the squadron's PTs were detached in January 1944, and went south again for duty in the ill-fated Anzio landing. Lieut. General Mark Clark, commanding the Fifth American Army, wanted the boats for water-taxi duty between the main American lines near Naples and the Anzio beachhead, thirty miles south of Rome. Usually the taxi runs were dull for sailors of the PT temperament, but not always.

On the morning of January 28th, General Clark and some of his staff boarded Lieut. (jg) George Patterson's 201 at the mouth of the Volturno River, and in company with 216 set sail for Anzio, seventy-five miles to the north.

Twenty-five miles south of Anzio, the minesweeper *Sway* patrolled the southern approaches to the beachhead. The captain had just been warned that enemy airplanes were attacking Anzio, and he knew that the Germans often coordinated air and E-boat strikes, so when he saw two small boats ripping along at high speed and coming down the sun's track, he challenged them by blinker light.

Without reducing speed, Lieut. Patterson answered with a six-inch light, too small a light for that distance in the daylight. Besides, the signalmen on the *Sway* were partly blinded by the glare of the sun, just rising behind the 201.

Sway's guns opened fire. Lieut. Patterson fired an emergency recognition flare, but it burst directly in the face of the sun, and the *Sway's* bridge crew missed the second friendly signal from the torpedo boat. The 201 even reduced speed as a further friendly gesture, but the slower speed only made the boat a better target.

The next shot hit the boat in the charthouse, wounding Lieut. Patterson and his executive officer, Ensign Paul R. Benson, and killing an officer passenger and a sailor.

"Let's get the hell out of here," suggested General Clark.

Ensign Benson, though wounded, took the wheel from the sagging skipper and zigzagged the boat away at high speed back toward Naples, until he was out of range of the *Sway's* batteries. A few miles down the coast the crew of 201 transferred dead and wounded to a British minesweeper.

The *Sway* still stood between the boat and Anzio, but General Clark wanted to go to the Anzio beach, so the 201 crept back at a peaceful-looking speed and spoke up from long distance with a bigger light. The sun was higher, *Sway's* signalmen read the message, and the skipper waved them by.

Lieut. Commander Barnes still restlessly experimented with armaments and tactics, looking for a combination of weapons and methods that would counter the dangerous weapons of the F-lighters. Rocket launchers were being mounted on landing craft, and the small vessels were delivering devastating ripples on enemy beaches. Their firepower was all out of proportion to the size of the craft. A few PTs were playing around with rocket launchers in the Pacific. It's worth at least a try, thought Lieut. Commander Barnes.

On the night of February 18th, 1944, Barnes went out in Lieut. (jg) Page H. Tullock's 211, with Lieut. Robert B. Reader's 203 and Lieut. (jg) Robert D. McLeod's 202.

As Lieut. Commander Barnes tells the story:

"I saw a small radar target come out from behind the peninsula and head over toward one of the small islands south of Giglio. Thinking it might be an F-lighter, I ordered rocket racks loaded.

"He must have seen us, because whatever it was — probably an E-boat — speeded up and ducked into the island before we could make contact. That presented the first difficulty of a rocket installation. There we were with the racks all loaded and the safety pins out. The weather had picked up a little, and getting those pins back in the rockets and the racks unloaded was going to be a touchy job in the pitch dark on wet, tossing decks. I decided to leave them there for a while to see what would happen.

"About midnight it started to kick up a good

deal more. I had just about decided that whatever it was we were looking for wasn't going to show up, and I was getting pretty worried about the rockets heaving out of the racks and rolling around in a semiarmed condition on deck. I decided to take one last turn around our patrol area and head for the barn.

"On our last southerly leg we picked up a target coming north at about eight knots, and I closed right away, thinking to spend all our rockets on whatever it was. As we got closer, it appeared to be two small targets in column—a conclusion which I later used as an outstanding example of 'Don't trust your interpretation of radar too blindly.'

"Just about the time we got to the 1,000-yard firing range the lookouts started reporting vessels everywhere, all the way from our port back around to our starboard bow. I had arranged the other two boats on either side in line abreast and ordered them to stand by to fire on my order over the radio. I gave the order and we all let go together.

"During the eleven seconds the rockets were in flight nobody fired a shot, but a couple of seconds after the rockets landed what seemed like a dozen enemy craft opened up. The formation was probably three or four F-lighters escorted by two groups of E-boats. We had passed through the two groups of escorts on our way to our firing position.

"Now it was time to turn away, and as my boat

turned to the right we found that the 202 was steaming right into the convoy. To avoid collision we had to turn back and parallel the 202.

"Just at that time the engines on my boat started to labor and unbelievably coughed and died—all three of them. We were smack dab in the center of the whole outfit, with the enemy shooting from all sides. . . . The volume was terrific.

"The 203 had lost all electric power, including the radar and compass lights. She saw the two of us off our original course and came back to join us, making a wide circle at high speed and laying smoke. It is impossible to say exactly what happened; the melee was too terrific.

"The 202 had a jammed rudder which they were able to clear. She eventually got out by ducking around several vessels, passing as close as 100 yards. The 203 likewise got out by ducking in and out of the enemy formation, but we on the 211 just sat there helpless, watching the whole show.

"This business lasted for at least four or five minutes and even the shore batteries came into illuminate with starshells. Fortunately, there was enough smoke in the air to keep the issue confused. That confusion was the only thing that saved us.

"None of our boats was using guns at all, and it was obvious that the enemy was frightfully confused with us weaving through the formation. They were hard at work shooting each other up. I am sure they sank at least one of the E-boats, because several minutes later they started firing again off to the north, and there was a large gasoline fire in the channel which burned for a long time.

"We got clear by the simple process of just sitting still and letting the enemy pass around us and continue north.

"I finally got one engine engaged and went to our rendezvous which was only a couple of miles away, but by the time I got there I could just see the other two boats, on the radar screen, leaving. I tried to call them back, but I couldn't get a soul and waited around for some time thinking they would come back. They didn't, however, and went on back individually, for which they got a little private hell from me later.

"I had no alternative but to go back myself. I expected to find the other two boats pretty well shot up, as it was a miracle that we weren't lost ourselves. Strangely enough, I found that they were not damaged, and except for the fantastic coincidence of all three of us being more or less disabled simultaneously, we were OK."

Apparently, the rockets did no damage, and further installation of rocket racks on his PTs was firmly rejected by Lieut. Commander Barnes.

The American PT commander was not the only one concerned about the heavy ordnance of the F-lighters. Captain J. F. Stevens of the British Navy's Coastal Forces in the Mediterranean said:

"While coastal forces are the most suitable forces to operate in mined areas, the enemy has so strengthened his escorts and armed his shipping that our coastal craft find themselves up against considerably heavier metal. Furthermore, the enemy's use of F-lighters of shallow draft does not provide good torpedo targets. Everything that can be done to improve our chances of successful attack is being done. Torpedoes will, if possible, be fired at even shallower settings. Meanwhile, if they cannot achieve destruction, coastal forces will harry the enemy and endeavour to cause him the utmost possible alarm, damage, and casualties."

Officers at La Maddalena gave longer thought to the problem and came up with an idea called Operation Gun.

Lieut. Commander Barnes' combined operation – the plan to use American radar for scouting and conning heavier-armed British boats to targets – had been a promising beginning, but even the MBG gunboats were not a real match for the F-lighters.

Commander Robert A. Allan, British Commandant of the Sardinia base, cut three landing craft out of the British amphibious fleet and armed them with 4.7 naval guns and 40-mm. autocannon. The landing craft were big, flat-bottomed tubs, wonderful platforms for the hard-hitting 4.7 inchers. To man the guns, he assigned crack gunners of the Royal Marine Artillery.

Commander Allan organized an interesting task

force around the three landing-craft gunboats (designated LCGs) as his main battle line. They were screened against E-boat attack by British torpedo boats, and controlled by the radar-equipped American PT scouting force.

Commander Allan himself went out on the first sweep of his beefed-up inshore patrol on the night of March 27th. He rode Lieut. (jg) Thaddeus Grundy's PT 218, so that he could use American radar to assign targets to his gunboats and give them opening salvo ranges and bearings by remote control.

When the gunboat battle line arrived off San Vicenzo, south of Leghorn, a scouting group of two PTs, under Lieut. Dubose, went off on a fast sweep, looking for targets. At 10 P.M. the PTs had found six F-lighters going south, and Commander Allan brought his main battle force up quickly to intercept them.

At 11 P.M. Lieut. Dubose sharply warned the main force that two destroyers were escorting the lighters on the seaward side. "I am preparing to attack the destroyers," he added.

Commander Allan continues the story: "Until he carried out this attack, it was not possible for us to engage the convoy, as our starshells being fired inshore over the target [to illuminate the F-lighters for the gunboats] would illuminate us for the escorting destroyers which were even farther to seaward than we were. Fire was therefore withheld during several anxious minutes."

During this ten-minute wait for the PT scouts to take on the destroyers, both the German forces, escort and convoy, came on Commander Allan's radar screen.

The PT scouts crept to within 400 yards before firing torpedoes, and ran away behind heavy smoke. Nevertheless, the destroyers laid down such a heavy fire that they hit 214, even in the smoke screen, wounding the engineer of the watch, Joseph F. Grossman, MoMM2c, and damaging the center engine. Grossman ignored his wounds and tended the stricken engine until it was running well again, staying below with his engines until the boat was out of danger.

The skippers of the scouting PTs heard the usual large explosions on one of the destroyers and hoped they had scored but couldn't be sure. Hit or no hit, the destroyers reversed course and ran up the coast, abandoning their convoy—an unthinkable act of cowardice for Allied escorts.

Sunk or run off, it was all the same to Commander Allan, who wanted only a free hand with the F-lighters. When the destroyers were gone, he passed radar ranges and bearings to the gunboats, and the Royal Marines lit up the night over the convoy with a perfect spread of starshells.

Startled gunners on the F-lighters, unused to this kind of treatment in waters where vessels with 4.7-inch guns had never dared venture before, took the lights for plane flares and fired wildly into the clouds.

The Royal Marine gunners took their time for careful aim under the bright glare of the slowly sinking magnesium lights. At the first salvo, one of the F-lighters blew up with a tremendous explosion. Within ten minutes three F-lighters were burning briskly. The gunboats spread out and pinned the surviving boats against the beach while the Marine artillerymen methodically pounded them to scrap.

"Of the six F-lighters destroyed," says Commander Allan, "two, judging by the impressive explosions, were carrying petrol, two ammunition, and one a mixed cargo of both."

With what sounds like a note of wistful disappointment, Commander Allan added: "The sixth sank without exploding."

The Operation Gun Task Force sortied again on the night of April 24th. The coastal waters around the Tuscan Archipelago were swarming with traffic that night. Early in the evening the gunboats blew two F-lighters out of the water. Burning debris, cascading from the sky after the explosions, set fires on the beach.

Shortly afterward the Marine sharpshooters picked off a tug and three more F-lighters.

Radar picked up still another group and starshell from the gunboats showed that they were three flak lighters—medium-size craft powerfully armed as antiaircraft escorts for daylight convoys. The Royal Marine gunners smacked their first salvos into two of the flak lighters, which burned in a fury of exploding ammunition.

The third lighter poured an astonishing volume of fire at the unarmored gunboats, and Commander Allan, in PT 218, made a fast run at the enemy to draw fire away from his gunboats. The Marines put a shell into the flak lighter, and it ran off behind smoke, but the 209 led a charge through the smoke, fired off its fish, caught the flak ship squarely amidships, and blew it in two.

Lieut. Dubose's scouting torpedo boats found a convoy escorted by a flak lighter, but at that moment the gunboats were engaged in another fight, so rather than break up the show of the main battle line, the PTs attacked the enemy themselves. At least one of three fish connected, for the flak lighter blew up in a jarring explosion.

Ashore, fifty miles away at Bastia, squadron mates sat outdoors to watch the flash and glare of the all-night battle against the eastern sky. Things were just threatening to get dull after midnight when shore radio at Bastia called Commander Allan with a radar-contact report of an Axis convoy between the gunboats and Corsica. The PTs got there first and found two destroyers and an E-boat in column.

When the PTs were still 2,500 yards away—too far for a good torpedo shot from a small boat —the destroyers fired a starshell. PT 202 was ready for just that emergency. A sailor standing by with a captured five-star recognition flare fired the correct answering lights and calmed the enemy's nerves.

The PTs moved in under the guise of friends and fired four fish at 1,700 yards. As they ran away they felt a violent underwater explosion, so they claimed a possible hit.

On this one wild night of action Commander Allan's strange little navy had, without damage to itself, sunk five of the formidable F-lighters, four heavily armed flak lighters, and a tug; scored a possible torpedo hit on a destroyer; and pulled a dozen German prisoners from the water.

Hearts of the PT sailors were lifted with joy in May 1944, when the Mark XIII torpedoes began to trickle into their bases and the heavy old-fashioned torpedo tubes were replaced with light launching racks that gave the boats badly needed extra bursts of speed. More boats had been arriving, too, and eventually there were three PT squadrons working out of Sardinia and Corsica.

As torpedomen installed the new fish and the new launching rigs, a PT skipper rubbed his hands and said: "Wait till we get a good target now.

These Mark Thirteens are going to sweep these waters clean."

Lieut. Eugene A. Clifford, in 204, led two other PTs in the first attack with the new torpedoes on the night of May 18th in the Tuscan Archipelago. The PTs had two flak lighters on their radarscopes. Determined to try out the new torpedoes, they bored through the massive barrage from the flak lighters' antiaircraft guns, firing from 1,000 yards.

One of the highly vaunted Mark XIII's made a typical Mark VIII run and hit the 204 in the stern. Fortunately, when this Mark XIII goofed, it really goofed, so it did not explode, but punched through the PT's skin and lodged its warhead inside. Its body dangled in the PT's wake, like a suckerfish clamped to a shark's tail.

Lewis H. Riggsby, TM2c, went into the lazaret to stuff towels into the vanes of the impeller to keep the torpedo from arming and exploding.

The flak lighters chased the PTs and hit 204 with 20-mm fire, but the boat escaped behind smoke, one of the famous Mark XIII torpedoes bobbing and dangling from the stern.

Dominating the Tuscan Archipelago, within sight of the Italian mainland, is the island of Elba, first home of Napoleon in exile. The island attracted the Allies, because big guns on the point closest to the mainland could reach the coastal road and also close off the inshore passage to coastal craft. Once Elba was in Allied hands, southbound Axis land traffic might be chased a few miles inland to less-developed mountain roads, and sea traffic would certainly be squeezed into the thirty miles of water between two Allied bases at Elba and Corsica.

One problem annoyed the planners of the Elba landings. What to do for naval support? The waters around Elba were probably the most heavily mined on the Italian Coast, and deep-draft ships could not be risked there. But then, hadn't PTs been scooting about the coast of Elba for nine months?

On the night between June 16th and 17th thirty-seven PTs joined other shallow-draft vessels of the Coastal Force to support landings of Senegalese troops of the French Ninth Colonial Division, plus mixed elements from other Allied forces.

Five PTs approached the northern coast at midnight, and about a half mile from shore put 87 French raiders in the water in rubber rafts. The five PTs joined another quintet at the farthest northeast point of Elba, the point closest to the mainland.

At 2 A.M. three of the ten PTs went roaring along the northern coast, smoke generators wide open and smoke pots dropping over the side in a steady stream. When the shoreline was sealed off behind a 16,000-yard curtain of smoke, four more PTs moved down the seaward side, with loudspeakers blaring the sounds of a great fleet of landing craft. The PTs launched occasional ripples of rockets at the beach to imitate a preinvasion shore bombardment.

The three remaining PT skippers carried on a lively radio exchange, straining their imaginations to invent a torrent of orders for an imaginary invasion armada.

Searchlights from the beach swept the water, looking for a hole in the screen. Land guns on the shore and in the mountains to the west poured shells into the smoke screen, thus pinpointing themselves nicely for an Allied air strike that slipped in just before dawn.

At the true landing beach on the south coast, Lieut. (jg) Eads Poitevent, Jr., captain of the 211, was posted as radar picket to guide landing craft ashore. He was alarmed when he saw a radar target creep out of the harbor at Marina de Campo. He could not attack without alerting the beach, and yet the oncoming enemy vessel had to be kept away from the landing flotilla at any cost.

Poitevent boldly sailed close to the target — an E-boat — and made friendly looking signals on a blinker light. He eased off in a direction away from the convoy, luring the patrol into harmless waters. It took him fifteen minutes to tease the E-boat off the scene and return to his duties.

The E-boat would not stay away, however, and in its aimless wanderings it blundered across the path of a PT with a deckload of British commandos destined for a preinvasion landing. The commandos slipped over the side, three-quarters of a mile farther out than they had planned, and silently paddled their rubber boats successfully to the beach, around the lackadaisacal enemy patrol.

Another PT saw the E-boat also, and thinking it was a friendly, tried to form up in column. Lieut. (jg) Harold J. Nugent, on 210, who was following the bumbling drama on radar, broke radio silence just long enough to cheep the smallest of warnings to his squadron mate. The E-boat crew incredibly fumbled about those waters, teeming with Allied boats, for most of the night and never lost their happy belief that they were alone with the stars and the sea.

PT radarscopes now showed a more interesting target. Coming right up the patrol line was something big, in fact, a formation of big ships, so PT skippers prepared for a torpedo attack. They held back, however, for full identification of the targets, because the ships could just possibly be the invasion flotilla, slightly off course.

At 400 yards, Nugent challenged the approaching formation by blinker. The nearest vessel answered correctly, and a few seconds later repeated the correct code phrase for the period.

Lieut. Nugent continues:

"Being convinced that the ships were part of the invasion convoy which had probably become lost, I called to my executive officer, Lieut. (jg) Joel W. Bloom, to be ready to look up the ships' correct position in our copy of the invasion plan. I brought the 210 up to the starboard side of the nearest ship, took off my helmet, put the megaphone to my mouth and called over 'What ship are you?'

"I shall never forget the answer.

"First there was a string of guttural words, followed by a broadside from the ship's two 88-mm. guns and five or six 20-mm. guns. The first blast carried the megaphone away and tore the right side off a pair of binoculars that I was wearing around my neck. It also tore through the bridge of the boat, jamming the helm, knocking out the bridge engine controls, and scoring a direct hit on the three engine emergency cutout switches which stopped the engines.

"I immediately gave the order to open fire, and though we were dead in the water and had no way of controlling the boat, she was in such a position as to deliver a full broadside.

"After a few minutes of heavy fire, we had reduced the firepower of the closest ship to one wildly wavering 20-mm. and one 88-mm. cannon which continued to fire over our heads throughout the engagement.

"It was easy to identify the ships, as the scene was well lighted with tracers. They were three ships traveling in a close V, an E-boat in the center with an F-lighter on either flank.

"We were engaging the F-lighter on the starboard flank of the formation. As the ships started to move toward our stern the injured F-lighter screened us from the fire of the other two ships, so I gave the order to cease fire.

"In the ensuing silence we clearly heard screams and cries from the F-lighter.

"Two members of our engine-room crew, who were topside as gun loaders during battle, were sent to the engine room to take over the chief engineer's duties, for I was sure he was dead or wounded. However, he had been working on the engines throughout the battle and had already found the trouble. We immediately got under way.

"We found out, however, that our rudder was jammed in a dead-ahead position, but by great good fortune we were headed directly away from the enemy, so I dropped a couple of smoke pots over the side and we moved off. The enemy shifted its fire to the smoke pots, and we lay to and started repairs.

"Much to our surprise, we found that none of us had even been wounded, but the boat had absorbed a great deal of punishment. A burst of 20 mm. had zipped through the charthouse, torn the chart table to bits, knocked out the lighting system, and detuned and scarred the radio and radar. Another burst had gone through the engine room, damaged control panels, torn the hull. All hits, however, were above the waterline. Turrets, turret lockers, ventilators, and the deck were holed.

"We called the 209 alongside, and sent off a radio report to the flagship on the action and the direction in which the ships retired."

Lieut. Nugent learned from the skipper of the 209 that his boat had been hit only twice, but one of the shells had scored a direct hit on a 40-mm. gun loader and killed him instantly.

The tall, black warriors from French Senegal swept over the island in two days of brisk fighting and Elba was Allied. The sea roads to the south were blocked, and PT action shifted to the north, to the Ligurian Sea, the Gulf of Genoa, and the lovely blue waters off the Côte d'Azur.

7.

The War in Europe:

English Channel

IN ENGLAND, as May 1944 turned into June, it didn't take a genius to know that something big was afoot. Military traffic choked the roads leading to the Channel seacoast and the coastal villages. Troops were in battle dress, officers were grim faced, all hands hustled about on the thousands of mysterious errands that presage an offensive. Everybody knew it was the Big Landing — the assault on Fortress Europe—but where?

Motor Torpedo Boat Squadron Two, under Lieut. Commander John Bulkeley (with only three boats this was the smallest squadron ever organized), had helped to make the decision where to land. Assigned to the Office of Strategic Services — America's cloak-and-dagger outfit for all kinds of secret business — Squadron Two had run a ferry service between England and the enemy-occupied continent to deliver secret agents, saboteurs, spies, resistance officers, and couriers for the governments in exile.

The sailors of Squadron Two carried out their

orders, of course, but on some of their errands they could mutter the old Navy adage: "I may have to take it, but I don't have to like it."

For example, the night they were sent across the Channel to land on the Normandy shore, there to scoop up several bucketfuls of sand. The crews grumbled about taking their fragile craft under the guns of Hitler's mighty Western Wall just to fill the First Sea Lord's sandbox.

They did not find out, until long after that night, why they were sent to play with shovels and buckets on the Normandy beach. A scientist who claimed to know the beaches well – beaches that had already been picked for the Normandy landings – said that they were made of spongy peat covered with a thin layer of sand, and that Allied trucks and tanks would bog down helplessly on the soft strand, once they left the hard decks of the landing craft.

The samples brought back by the PT sailors proved that the scientist didn't know sand from shinola about Normandy beach conditions, and the operation went ahead as planned.

On June 6, 1944, the first waves of American and British troops landed on Omaha and Utah beaches and began the long slugging match with Marshal Erwin Rommel's Nazis to twist Normandy out of German hands.

During the landings proper, PTs were used as

anti-E-boat screens, but made their biggest contribution by dousing flare floats dropped by German aircraft to guide their night bombers.

At the beginning the assigned duties of the PTs were not heavy, but there is always work for a fleet of small, handy armed boats in a big amphibious operation.

On June 8th, for instance, as the destroyer *Glennon* jockeyed about off the Saint Marcouf Islands, north of Utah Beach, getting ready to bombard a shore battery, she struck a mine astern. One minesweeper took the damaged destroyer under tow, and another went ahead to sweep a clear escape channel. Just before 9 A.M., the destroyer-escort *Rich* closed the ships, and the skipper asked if he could help. The captain of the *Glennon* answered: "Negative; clear area cautiously, live mines."

Too late. A heavy explosion stopped the *Rich* dead in the water. A second explosion tore away fifty feet of the stern. A third mine exploded forward. The destroyer-escort was a shambles, its keel broken and folded in a V. The superstructure was festooned with a grisly drapery of bodies and parts of bodies.

PTs rallied around the *Rich* to take survivors from the deck or from the mine-filled waters around the shattered vessel. Crewmen on the 508 saw a sailor bobbing by in the sea, and the bowman picked up a heaving line to throw to his rescue.

The man in the water calmly refused assistance.

"Never mind the line," he said, "I have no arms to catch it."

The PT skipper, Lieut. Calvin R. Whorton, dove into the icy Channel waters, but the armless sailor had gone to the bottom.

The *Rich* followed him in fifteen minutes, with 79 of the crew. Seventy-three survivors were wounded.

The *Glennon* itself went aground, and two days later a German shore battery put two salvos aboard. The destroyer rolled over and sank.

American soldiers ashore pushed rapidly northwestward along the coast of the Cherbourg Peninsula, to capture the port of Cherbourg, sorely needed as a terminal to replace the temporary harbor behind a jury-rig breakwater of sunken ships at the landing beaches. The Nazi garrison at Cherbourg put up a last-ditch stand, however, and on June 27th, forts on the outer breakwater and a few coastal batteries still held out.

The Navy sent a curiously composed task force to reduce the forts. With the destroyer *Shubrick*, the Navy sent six PTs to deal with the holdout Germans. It is hard to understand what PTs were expected to accomplish against heavy guns behind concrete casemates. Perhaps the reputation of the PT commander had overpowered the judgment of the Navy brass, for it was none other than Lieut. Commander John Bulkeley, hero of the MacArthur rescue run and the New Guinea blockade, come to try his mettle in European waters.

Leaving four PTs with the destroyer as a screen, Bulkeley, in 510, with 521 in company, cruised by the forts and sprayed them with machine guns at 150-yard range. The stubborn Nazis poured out a stream of 88-mm. shells and hit 521 hard enough to stop her dead for five minutes while a motor machinist mate made frantic repairs. Lieut. Commander Bulkeley ran rings around the stalled craft, laying a doughnut of smoke around her for a screen.

The *Shubrick* herself was taking near misses from shore batteries, so the skipper recalled the PTs and departed the scene. The two "bombardment" PTs followed suit, having accomplished little except to exercise the crew. Fortunately no American sailors were hurt in this most inappropriate use of PT capabilities.

Even after the Allies had taken the whole Normandy coast, the Germans clung to the offshore Channel Islands of Jersey, Alderney, Guernsey, and Sark. On Jersey, they maintained a base for small craft which made annoying nightly sorties.

To seal off the Jersey base, the Navy ordered PT Squadrons Thirty and Thirty-four to patrol nightly

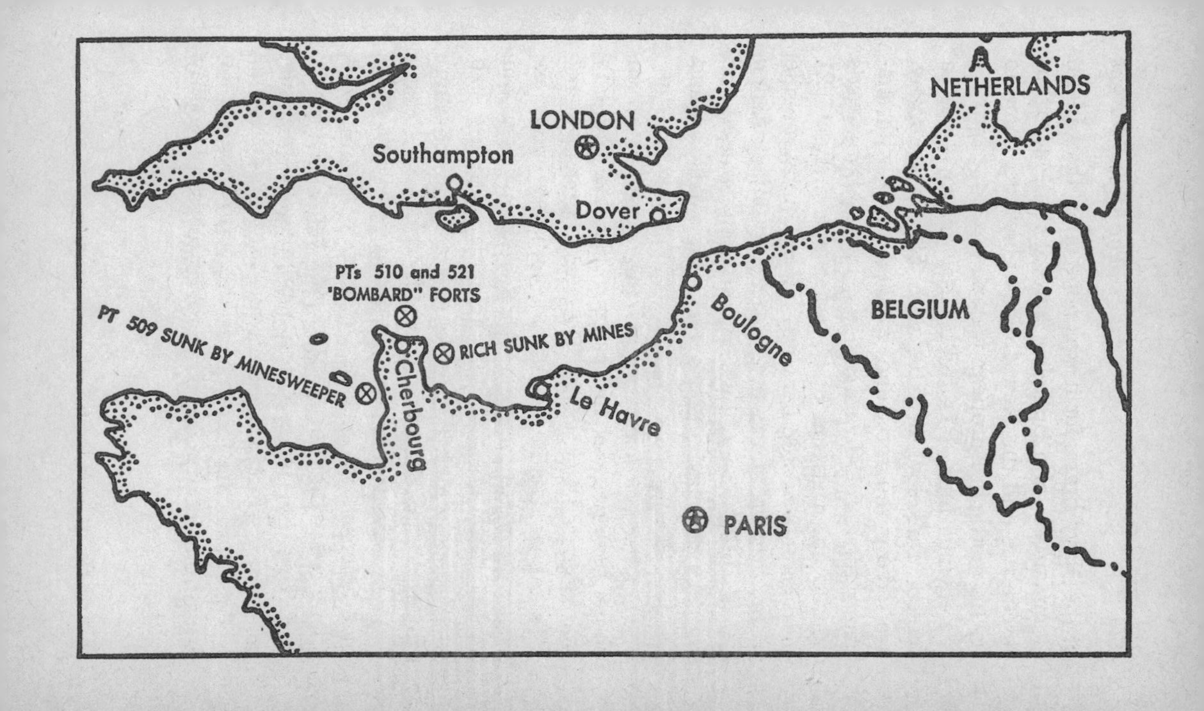
NETHERLANDS
LONDON
Southampton
Dover
PTs 510 and 521
"BOMBARD" FORTS
PT 509 SUNK BY MINESWEEPER
RICH SUNK BY MINES
Cherbourg
Boulogne
BELGIUM
Le Havre
PARIS

from Cherbourg to the Channel Islands in the company of a destroyer escort for backstop firepower and for radar scouting.

On the night between August 8th and 9th, the *Maloy* and five PTs were patrolling west of Jersey. The weather was good all night, but shortly before dawn a thick fog settled over the sea. At 5:30 A.M. the radar watch on the *Maloy* picked up six German minesweepers.

Lieut. H. J. Sherertz, as the officer in tactical command of the PT patrol, was riding *Maloy* to use its superior radar. He dispatched three PTs from the northern end of the scouting line to attack the Germans. The skipper of PT 500, one of the north scout group, was Lieut. Douglas Kennedy, now editor of *True* magazine. Blinded by the peasouper, the PTs fired torpedoes by radar, but missed.

Thirty minutes later, Lieut. Sherertz vectored the southern pair of torpedo boats to the attack. The 508 and 509 approached the firing line through the fog at almost 50 knots. Lieut. Harry M. Crist, a veteran of many PT battles in Pacific waters and skipper of 509, risked one fish by radar aim from 500 yards. Lieut. Whorton (the officer who had tried in vain to save the armless sailor of the *Rich*) couldn't fire, because his radar conked out at the critical moment, so the PTs circled and Lieut. Crist conned the 508 by radio. The boats fired but missed.

As they came about to circle again, Whorton reported that he heard heavy firing break out between the other PT and a minesweeper, but he couldn't shoot because his buddies were between him and the Germans. Whorton lost the 509 in the swirling fog, and when he came around again, everybody had disappeared. He searched almost an hour and returned to the *Maloy* on orders of Lieut. Sherertz, because his burned-out radar made his search ineffective.

The 503 and the 507 took up the search for their missing comrades. At 8 A.M. they picked up a radar target in the St. Helier roadstead at Jersey, and closed to 200 yards. The fog lifted briefly and unveiled a minesweeper dead ahead and on a collision course. The 503 fired a torpedo, and both boats raked the enemy's decks, but suffered hard punishment themselves from the enemy's return fire. Before the boats escaped from the enemy waters, two PT sailors were killed and four wounded on 503, and one wounded on 507.

The next day a search plane found the body of a sailor from the 509, and ten days later a bullet-riddled section of the hull was found floating in the Channel. It was not until after the war that the fate of the 509 was learned from the sole survivor, a liberated prisoner of war named John L. Page, RdM3c. Here is his story:

"After firing one torpedo by radar, the 509 circled and came in for a gunnery run. I was in the charthouse on the radar. Lieut. (jg) John K. Pavlis was at the wheel. I remember we were moving fast and got pretty close before receiving return fire. When it came it was heavy and accurate.

"One shell burst in the charthouse, knocking me out. When I came to, I was trying to beat out flames with my hands. I was wounded and the boat was on fire, but I pulled the detonator switch to destroy the radar and then crawled on deck.

"The bow of our boat was hung up on the side of a 180-foot minesweeper. From the deck of the enemy sweeper, Germans were pouring in small-arms fire and grenades. Everything aft of the cockpit was burning. I struggled forward through the bullets and bursting grenades to the bow—I have no idea how long that journey took—and the Germans tossed me a line. I had just enough strength to take it and they hauled me aboard."

The Germans stretched Page out on the deck and attacked the PT's carcass with crowbars, frantically trying to pry themselves loose from its clutches. Just as the PT broke loose, it exploded with a tremendous roar.

"I couldn't see it," says Page, "but I felt the heat and the blast."

Free of the PT, the minesweeper ran for the shelter of home base at St. Helier. The Germans carried Page back to the crew's quarters to tend his wounds. He had a broken right arm and leg, thirty-seven bullet and shrapnel holes in his body, and a large-caliber slug in his lungs. While they were working on him they were carrying in their own dead and wounded.

"I managed to count the dead. There were fifteen of them and a good number of wounded. It's difficult to estimate how many, because they kept milling around. I guess I conked out for a while. The first thing I remember is a first-aid man putting a pack on my back and arm. Then I could hear the noise of the ship docking.

"After they removed their dead and wounded, they took me ashore at St. Helier. They laid me out on the dock for quite a while, and a couple of civilians — I found out later they were Gestapo agents — tried to question me, but they saw I was badly shot up, so they didn't try to question me further."

Page was taken to a former English hospital at St. Helier, where skillful German surgeons performed many operations — he couldn't remember how many — to remove dozens of bullets and fragments from every part of his body. The final operation was on December 27, 1944.

While he was in the hospital, the bodies of three of his shipmates washed ashore on Jersey. The British Red Cross took over the bodies and buried them with military honors.

Page was regularly annoyed by Gestapo men, but he said: "I found that being very correct and stressing the fact that my government didn't permit me to answer was very effective. They tried a few times and finally let me alone."

Page was liberated on May 8, 1945.

The Channel Island battles were vicious and inconclusive, in a sense, but the German gadflies stayed more and more in port — became more and more timid when they did patrol. Nightly sweeps of the PT-destroyer escort teams bottled up the German boats and cleared the Channel waters for the heavy traffic serving the voracious appetite of the armies on the continent.

8.

The War in Europe:

Azure Coast

AFTER Allied troops had chopped out a good firm foothold on the northwestern coast of France, the Allied Command found that the Channel ports were not enough to handle the immense reserve of men and materials waiting in America to be thrown into the European battle. Another port was needed, preferably one on the German flank in order to give the enemy another problem to fret about.

Marseilles was the choice, with the naval base at Toulon to be taken in the same operation. The Allies set H-hour for 8 A.M. on August 15, 1944, and assembled their Mediterranean naval power in Italian ports. Among the destroyers assigned to the shore fire-support flotilla were ships of the Free Polish and Free Greek fleets.

Lieut. Commander Stanley Barnes, when he heard about these new comrades in arms, paraded his PTs past the Greek destroyer in daylight so that the Hellenic sailors could see what an American torpedo boat looked like. With a strong sense of history, Barnes remembered the Battle of Salamis, and he didn't want the Greeks to mistake his boats for Persians.

As it turned out, the first duty for the PTs was to be mistaken for what they were not.

With two British gunboats, a fighter director ship and three slow, heavily armed motor launches, PTs of Squadron Twenty-Two sailed from Corsica on August 14th, bound for the coast of France. This task unit was under the command of Lieut. Commander Douglas Fairbanks, Jr., the American movie star.

Three of the PTs were detached to sail for the northwest as an anti-E-boat patrol. Four others took 70 French commandos northwest to land at the Pointe des Deux Frères, in the beautiful Gulf of Napoule that washes the beach at Cannes. (The French commandos ran into a mine field ashore, were strafed by friendly planes, and captured by the Germans.)

The rest of the task unit sailed straight north, as though headed for Genoa, trailing balloons as radar targets, with the hope that the enemy would think a big invasion force was bound for the Italian seaport.

At Genoa, the phony flotilla turned west for the waters off Cannes and Nice, still trailing its radar target balloons. The launches and PTs maneuvered off Antibes, making as much of an uproar as pos-

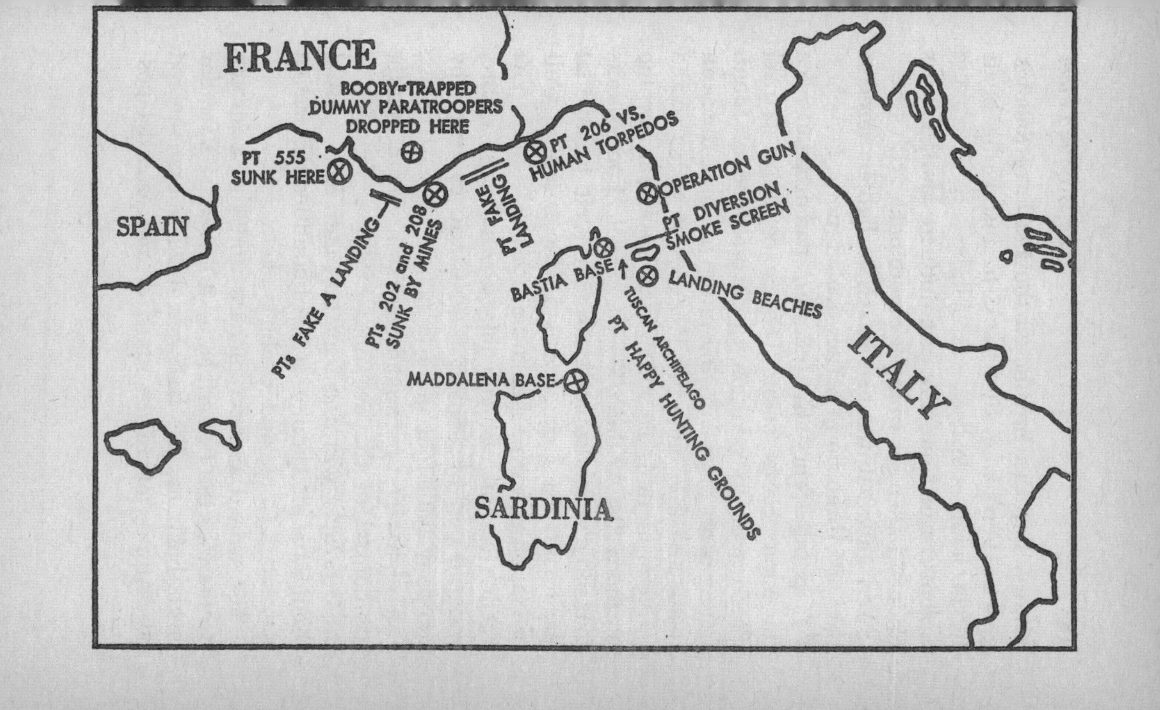
FRANCE
BOOBY-TRAPPED DUMMY PARATROOPERS DROPPED HERE
PT 555 SUNK HERE
SPAIN
PTs FAKE A LANDING
PTs 202 and 208 SUNK BY MINES
PT FAKE LANDING
PT 206 VS. HUMAN TORPEDOS
OPERATION GUN
PT DIVERSION SMOKE SCREEN
LANDING BEACHES
BASTIA BASE
TUSCAN ARCHIPELAGO
PT HAPPY HUNTING GROUNDS
MADDALENA BASE
ITALY
SARDINIA

sible, while the British gunboats bombarded the beach.

The minuscule fleet was delighted to hear from Radio Berlin that a massive Allied landing near Cannes had been pushed into the sea with heavy losses, and that Antibes and Nice had been bombarded by four large battleships.

Captain Henry C. Johnson, commanding the diversion groups, said: "The decoy screen proved effective as in addition to several enemy salvos falling short of or bursting in the air over the gunboats, the PTs and the launches were subjected to a considerable degree of large-caliber fire which passed well over them."

Happy with the confusion they had sown, the eastern diversion group sailed west to join a western task unit with a similar mission.

Off the Baie de la Ciotat, between Marseilles and the port of Toulon, the eastern group joined company with four more launches, 11 crash boats, and eight PTs of Squadron Twenty-Nine, under the control of the destroyer *Endicott*. Skipper of the destroyer was a sailor who might be expected to know a bit about a PT's capabilities. His name was Lieut. Commander John Bulkeley.

The armed motor launches and the destroyer bombarded the beach behind a screen of PTs. The crash boats trailed balloons, laid smoke screens, fired ripples of rockets at the beach, laid delayed-action bombs in shallow water to imitate frogmen at work, and broadcast noises of many landing craft. The crash boats hoped to give the impression of a convoy ten miles long and eight miles wide.

At 4 A.M. troop-carrier planes flew over the town of La Ciotat and dropped 300 booby-trapped dummy paratroopers.

Radio Berlin broadcast an alarm. "The Allies are landing forces west of Toulon and east of Cannes. Thousands of enemy paratroops are being dropped in areas northwest of Toulon."

With great bitterness, five hours later, Radio Berlin broadcast: "These paratroops were found later to be only dummies which had booby traps attached and which subsequently killed scores of innocent civilians. This deception could only have been conceived in the sinister Anglo-Saxon mind."

This complaint came from the nation that was the world's acknowledged master at the nasty and unmanly art of booby-trappery.

Radio Berlin continued: "Large assault forces have attempted to breach defenses west of Toulon, but as the first waves have been wiped out by mine fields, the rest lost heart and withdrew and returned to an area in the east."

For two more nights the deception forces shelled the beach and made noises like a mighty host.

For two days the Germans announced that the

main Allied intention was to take Toulon and Marseilles by direct assault, and talked of driving off an invasion force including five battleships.

Before sailing away after the last phony demonstration, Lieut. Commander Bulkeley broadcast a message, saying that the landings at La Ciotat would be postponed for a few days "because of the furious resistance on the beach," but that they would definitely come. The Germans reinforced the La Ciotat area with mobile artillery and infantry units, sorely needed elsewhere.

Radio Berlin, after the final demonstration, said: "An additional and futile attempt of the American forces to land large bodies of troops west of Toulon has failed miserably."

Lord Haw Haw, the English traitor who broadcast for the Axis, said: "The assault convoy was twelve miles long, but for the second time in three nights the Allies have learned of the determined resistance of the *Wehrmacht*, to their cost."

The Axis broadcasts had the unexpected result of terrifying crews of German warships ordered out to attack the "invasion fleet." Prisoners of war later reported that some of the ships would not sail because they had lost heart after listening to their own broadcast alarms.

Some ships did venture out, however, for one of the crash boats, retiring from the demonstration area after the final show, ran into two enemy corvettes – heavily armed escort vessels. The crash boat called loudly for help, and two antique British river gunboats, the *Aphis* and the *Scarab*, came running. The British and German ships battled for twenty minutes. Lieut. Commander Bulkeley's *Endicott*, already almost out of sight on the southern horizon, steamed back at flank speed and opened fire at seven and one-half-mile range. Fire was slow, however, for the *Endicott*, trying to imitate a large bombardment force earlier that night, had shot its five-inchers so fast that all but one breech block was fused from the heat. The one remaining gun shifted fire from one corvette to the other.

Two PTs, screening the destroyer, closed the corvettes to 300 yards and fired two fish, but missed. The *Endicott* also fired torpedoes, and the corvettes turned bow on to comb their tracks, thus masking their own broadside. The *Endicott* closed to 1,500 yards and raked the corvette decks with 20-mm. and 40-mm. autocannon, driving gunners from their stations.

The British gunboats and the destroyer pounded the now silent corvettes until they sank. The ships and PT boats picked up 211 prisoners from the *Nimet Allah*, a converted Egyptian yacht, and the *Capriolo*, a smartly rigged light warship taken from the Italian navy.

In southern waters the PTs had been immune to mines, but off the Mediterranean shores of France they suffered terribly from a new type of underwater menace.

Following standard PT practice of moving the base as close to the fighting front as possible, Lieut. Commander Barnes set up a boat pool in the Baie de Briande, near Saint Tropez, almost as soon as the troops went ashore. The boats were close to the fighting and ready for action, but their gas tanker didn't show up. By the evening of August 16th the boats were low on fuel, so the skippers puttered about the coast, running down rumors of gas tankers anchored here and there.

Lieut. (jg) Wesley Gallagher in 202, and Lieut. Robert Dearth in 218, set sail together to look for a tanker reported to be in the Gulf of Fréjus, fifteen miles to the northeast, the other side of Saint Tropez. At 11 P.M., as the boats were rounding the point of St. Aygulf to enter the harbor at Fréjus, the bow lookout on 202 sang out that he saw a boxlike object floating 150 yards dead ahead. The skipper turned out to sea to avoid it.

During the turn a mine tore the stern off the boat, blew stunned sailors into the water, and threw a column of water, smoke, and splinters hundreds of feet into the air. Four sailors jumped overboard to rescue their shipmates.

Lieut. Dearth brought the 218 over to pick up the swimming sailors and tried to approach the floating section of the 202 to take off survivors, but the stern of his boat was blown off in the stunning explosion of another mine.

The two skippers abandoned the shattered hulks of their boats. In the life rafts they held a muster. One man was missing and six men were wounded. Amazingly, the engineers of the watch on both boats survived, though they had been stationed right over blasts so powerful that heavy storage batteries had whizzed by them to land on the forecastle.

The sailors paddled shoreward. German planes were raiding the beach at that moment, and shrapnel from the antiaircraft barrage rained down on the rafts.

Shortly after midnight, the sailors landed on a rocky point chosen by the skippers because it looked least likely to be land mined. Lieut. Gallagher picked his way through a barbed-wire barricade along the beach and found a deserted and partly destroyed fisherman's cottage where the sailors lay low for the rest of the night, not knowing whether they had landed in friendly or enemy territory.

Soon after dawn the skippers made a tentative venture into the open. Half a mile from the cottage they ran into soldiers — American soldiers — who took over the wounded men and guided the other sailors to a Navy beachmaster who gave them a boat ride back to their base.

A week later, on August 24th, task-force commander Rear Admiral L. A. Davidson heard that the Port-de-Bouc in the Gulf of Fos, west of Marseilles and at the mouth of the Rhone Delta, had been captured by the French Underground. He ordered minesweepers to clear the gulf, and he sent Capitaine de Frégate M. J. B. Bataille, French naval liaison officer on his staff, to scout the shore around the harbor. Capt. Bataille rode to the gulf in Lieut. Bayard Walker's ill-fated PT 555.

The boat passed the minesweepers and came close aboard an American destroyer whose skipper notified Lieut. Walker that coastal shore batteries were still shooting near the mouth of the Gulf of Fos.

Lieut. Bayard reported: "It was decided that we could enter the Gulf of Fos, despite fire from enemy coastal batteries, since we presented such a small target."

So — as he put it — they "entered the bay cautiously."

One wonders how you go about entering a mine-filled bay, by an enemy shore battery, "cautiously."

The crew saw the French flag flying in a dozen places on the beach, and landed at Port-de-Bouc where they were welcomed by a cheering crowd, waving little French flags. Capt. Bataille met a fellow officer, French Navy Lieut. Granry, who had parachuted into the area several weeks before, in civilian clothes, and had organized a resistance cell to prevent demolition of the port when the Germans retreated. After a pleasant half-hour ashore, gathering information (Lieut. Walker spoke excellent French), the party re-embarked, set a two-man watch on the bow, and headed for sea at 29 knots.

"A few minutes later," said Lieut. Walker, "a terrific blast exploded beneath our stern, carrying away the 40-mm. gun and the gun crew and almost everything else up to the forward bulkhead of the engine room. . . . The four torpedoes were immediately jettisoned and we anchored with two anchors from separate lines."

Volunteers manned the life rafts to pick up the men in the water. They returned with a body, one uninjured sailor, and a man with a broken leg. Four other sailors were never found.

One of the rafts could not return to the boat because of strong currents, so Lieut. Stanley Livingston, a powerful swimmer, swam the 300 yards, towing the bitter end of a line patched together of all available manila, electric cable, halyards, and odds and ends, buoyed at intervals with life jackets. Sailors on the boat then pulled the raft alongside.

A French pilot boat and a fisherman in an open boat came out from the beach to help. Overhead, fighter planes, attracted by the explosion, took in the situation and set up an impromptu umbrella.

The sailor with the broken leg needed help. Lieut. Walker put him and the dead sailor's body into the fisherman's boat with the pharmacist's mate, and climbed in himself, as interpreter. They shoved off for Port-de-Bouc.

One hundred yards from the PT boat, Walker saw in the water a green line with green floats spaced every foot. He yelled a warning at the fisherman, but too late. A violent explosion lifted the boat in the air and threw the four men into the water.

Lieut. Walker came up under the boat and had to fight himself free of the sinking craft. He took stock. The dead sailor had disappeared forever. The pharmacist's mate, about sixty feet away, was shouting that he couldn't swim, so Walker went to the rescue. The injured man was hauled up to the bottom of the overturned boat where, in Walker's words, "He appeared to be comfortable."

The ordinary non-PT man might consider a perch on the bottom of an overturned and sinking fishing boat as being somewhat short of "comfortable" for a man with an unset broken leg.

"The situation seemed so good," continued Lieut. Walker in the same happy vein, "that I decided not to take off my pistol and belt. . . . The French pilot boat came to our rescue, and the injured man was put aboard without further harm. The fishermen's boat upended and sank as the last man let go."

Walker confessed to a tiny twinge of disappointment at this point in his narrative. A scouting float plane from the cruiser *Philadelphia* had landed near the shattered boat, and the PT officers had hoped to get off their message to the task-force commander, but the pilot took fright when the second mine went off under the fishing boat, and he left for home.

"We had two narrow escapes getting back to the PT boat," Lieut. Walker said. "I requested the pilot, Ensign Moneglia of the French Navy, to go between two sets of lines I could see, rather than back down and turn around as the majority seemed to wish. It proved to be the safe way between two mines."

The crew jettisoned all topside weights except one twin 50-caliber mount, so that they would have some protection against air attack.

Captain Bataille and Lieut. Livingston set out in a rubber boat for the town of Carro, at the eastern entrance of the Gulf of Fos, about five miles away. They were frantic to complete their mission by sending a message to the task-force commander, and they hoped to find an Army message center to relay their report that Port-de-Bouc was in French hands.

Two teams of bucket brigades bailed out the

leaking hulk, but the water gained on them steadily. At midnight the sailors jettisoned the radar and brought up confidential publications in a lead-weighted sack, ready to be heaved over if they had to abandon the boat. The off-duty bucket brigade had to share a few blankets, because the night was chilly.

About an hour after sunrise Captain Bataille and Lieut. Livingston returned from Carro in a fishing boat, followed by another. That brought the little flotilla to two pilot boats, two fishing boats, and a battered piece of a PT. The two message-bearers had been unable to find an Army radio.

Two of the boats passed lines to the PT to tow it ashore, and the other two went ahead with Captain Bataille and Lieut. Livingston in the bows, as lookouts for moored mines. They found so many on the road to Port-de-Bouc that the flotilla turned and headed for Carro, on Cape Couronne, instead.

At the Carro dock, the PT settled to the bottom. An abandoned house beside the dock was turned over to the homeless sailors, and the French Underground trotted up five Italian prisoners to do the dirty work of making the place presentable.

Best news in Carro was that the cruiser *Philadelphia* had just sent an officer ashore with a radio, to send out some news of possible targets along the shore. Lieut. Walker tracked down his colleague, and after bloody travail, finally sent off his message to the task-force commander that Port-de-Bouc was indeed in friendly hands, but that the harbor waters were still acting in a very unfriendly manner indeed.

Walker threw in a little bonus of the fact that 3,000 enemy troops were only a few kilometers away and that the French Underground fighters were afraid they might escape via Martigues. He relayed the resistance officer's plea for an air strike to break up the escape attempt long enough for American troops to arrive and sweep up the Germans.

Lieut. Walker adds a touching finale to his report:

"I had asked the pastor of the Catholic church at La Couronne, a village slightly more than a mile from Carro, to say a Mass on Sunday morning for the five men we had lost. A High Mass was celebrated in the church, crowded to the doors, at 10:30.

"The pastor and local people had gone to considerable trouble to decorate the church with French and American flags and flowers. The choir sang, despite the broken organ, and the *curé* gave a moving sermon in French. Four FFI [Underground] men, gotten up in a uniform of French helmets, blue shirts, and white trousers, stood as a guard of honor before symbolical coffins draped with American flags.

"After Mass our men fell in ranks behind a platoon of FFI, and followed by the whole town, we marched to the World War I monument. There a little ceremony was held and a wreath was placed in honor of the five American sailors.

"We were told that a collection was in the process of being taken up amongst the local people, in order to have a plaque made for the monument planned for their own dead in this war. The plaque will bear the names of the five Americans who gave their lives here for the liberation of France."

The people of La Couronne did not forget. In that tiny village, on the lonely coast at the mouth of the Rhone River, is a monument with a plaque reading: To Our Allies, Ralph W. Bangert, Thomas F. Devaney, John J. Dunleavy, Harold R. Guest, Victor Sippin.

One of the most brilliant Anglo-American teams was Lieut. R. A. Nagle's 559 and the British MTB 423, both under command of the dashing British Lieut. A. C. Blomfield.

During the night of August 24th, the marauding pair entered the harbor of Genoa to raise a bit of general hell. Off Pegli, about five miles from Genoa, they sighted what they thought was a destroyer, and put a torpedo into it. The vessel was only a harbor-defense craft, but a fair exchange for the one torpedo it cost.

Two nights later the pair jumped a convoy of three armed barges, and sank two of them. For the next nine nights they tangled almost hourly with F-lighters (four sunk), armed barges (eight sunk), and even a full-grown corvette, the UJ 2216, formerly the French *l'Incomprise,* which they riddled and sent to the bottom as the top prize of their 11-day spree.

Hunting got progressively meager as winter came on. PTs prowled farther afield and closer inshore in a ferocious search for targets. On November 17th, Lieut. B. W. Creelman's PT 311 pressed the search too far, hit a mine, and sank. Killed were the skipper and his executive officer and eight of the 13-man crew.

The last big fight of the American PTs with enemy surface craft came two nights later when Lieut. (jg) Charles H. Murphy's 308 and two British torpedo boats sank a thousand-ton German corvette, the UJ 2207, formerly the French *Cap Nord.*

The naval war was nearing its end for the Germans, and they turned to strange devices—human torpedoes, remote-control explosive boats, and semisuicide explosive boats. The remote-control craft didn't work any better for the Germans than they had for Americans in the Normandy landings. So it was, also, with the human torpedo.

Lieut. Edwin Dubose, on PT 206, on September 10th, spotted a human torpedo in the waters off the French-Italian frontier. The PT sank the torpedo and pulled the pilot from the water. With great insouciance, the pilot chatted with his rescuers and treacherously told them where to find and kill a comrade piloting another torpedo.

In those waters that same day, planes, PTs and bigger ships sank ten human torpedoes.

As naval resistance lessened, the Western Naval Task Force, under American Rear Admiral H. K. Hewitt, was broken up and redistributed. Many PTs were assigned to the Flank Force, Mediterranean. Since most of the ships in the force were French, the PTs came under the command of French Contre-Amiral Jaujard.

Because Mark XIIIs were arriving in good numbers — the torpedo targets were getting scarce — the French admiral authorized the PTs in his command to fire their old and unlamented Mark VIIIs into enemy harbors.

On the night of March 21st, PTs 310 and 312 fired four Mark VIIIs, from two miles, into the harbor of Savona, Italy. Three exploded on the beach.

The same boats, on April 4th, fired four at the resort town of San Remo. Two exploded, one of them with such a crash that it jarred the boats far out to sea.

On April 11th, the 313 and the 305 fired four into Vado, touching off one large explosion and four smaller ones.

The last three Mark VIIIs were fired from the 302 and the 305 on April 19th. Lieut. Commander R. J. Dressling, the squadron leader, launched them into Imperia where a single boom was heard.

"During these torpedoings of the harbors," said Dressling, "Italian partisans were rising against the Germans, and there is little doubt that the explosions of our torpedoes were taken by the enemy as sabotage attempts by the partisans. At no time were we fired on, despite the fact that we were well inside the range of enemy shore batteries."

Lieut. Commander Dressling thought that "to a small extent the actions assisted the partisans in taking over the Italian ports on April 27th."

The night after the Italian ports all fell to the Italian Underground, Admiral Jaujard, with a fine Gallic sense of the ceremonial, led his entire Flank Force, including PT Squadron Twenty-two, in a stately sweep of the Riviera coast. It was partly the last combat patrol and partly a victory parade.

Ten days later, on May 8th, the Germans surrendered and the war was over—the war was over in Europe, that is, for on the other side of the world the PTs were involved in the bitterest fighting yet.

PTs had operated in the Mediterranean for two years. The three squadrons lost four boats, five officers and 19 men killed in action, seven officers and 28 men wounded in action. They fired 354 torpedoes and claimed 38 vessels sunk, totaling 23,700 tons, and 49 damaged, totaling 22,600 tons. In joint patrols with the British they claimed 15 vessels sunk and 17 damaged.

9.

I Shall Return–

Round Trip by PT

WITH the whole of New Guinea and the island base at Morotai in Allied hands, the Philippine Islands were within reach of Allied fighter planes and it was time for General MacArthur to make good his promise.

There was a lot of mopping up to do around Morotai, however, because the taking of the island had been a typical MacArthur leapfrog job. Morotai was a small and lightly defended island, but twelve miles away was the big island of Halmahera, defended by 40,000 Japanese. MacArthur had jumped over it to continue his successful New Guinea policy of seizing bases between the Japanese and their home, then isolating the by-passed garrison with a naval blockade.

The best way to bottle up the Halmahera garrison was to call on the PT veterans of the New Guinea blockade, so the day after the landings on Morotai, September 16, 1944, the tenders *Oyster Bay* and *Mobjack*, with the boats of Squadrons Ten, Twelve, Eighteen, and Thirty-three, dropped anchor in Morotai roadstead. The first adventure of the Morotai PTs was the rescue, on the very day of their arrival, of a wounded Navy fighter pilot. (A full account of this is given at the end of Chapter 5.)

PT sailors sometimes wondered what the Stone Age people of Halmahera, people who fought with barbed ironwood spears, made of the strange war being fought in their waters by the white and yellow intruders from the twentieth century. Lieut. (jg) Roger M. Jones, skipper of PT 163, tells about an encounter that has probably entered the mythology of these pagan people.

In October 1944, Lieut. Jones's boat and the 171 left Morotai for a routine patrol to keep the bypassed Japanese of Halmahera from crossing to Morotai. In the six weeks since the landings, PTs had already sunk fifty Japanese barges, schooners, and luggers carrying troops and supplies.

During the New Guinea campaign, as the use of torpedoes shriveled for lack of suitable targets, the 163 had mounted an awesome battery of ten 50-caliber machine guns in twin mounts, two 20-mm., a 37-mm., a 40-mm. autocannon, and a 60-mm. mortar.

The night's problem was simple. Intelligence had told the PT skippers that there would be no friendlies in the patrol area on the west coast of Halmahera—no friendlies at all. "Shoot anything that moves."

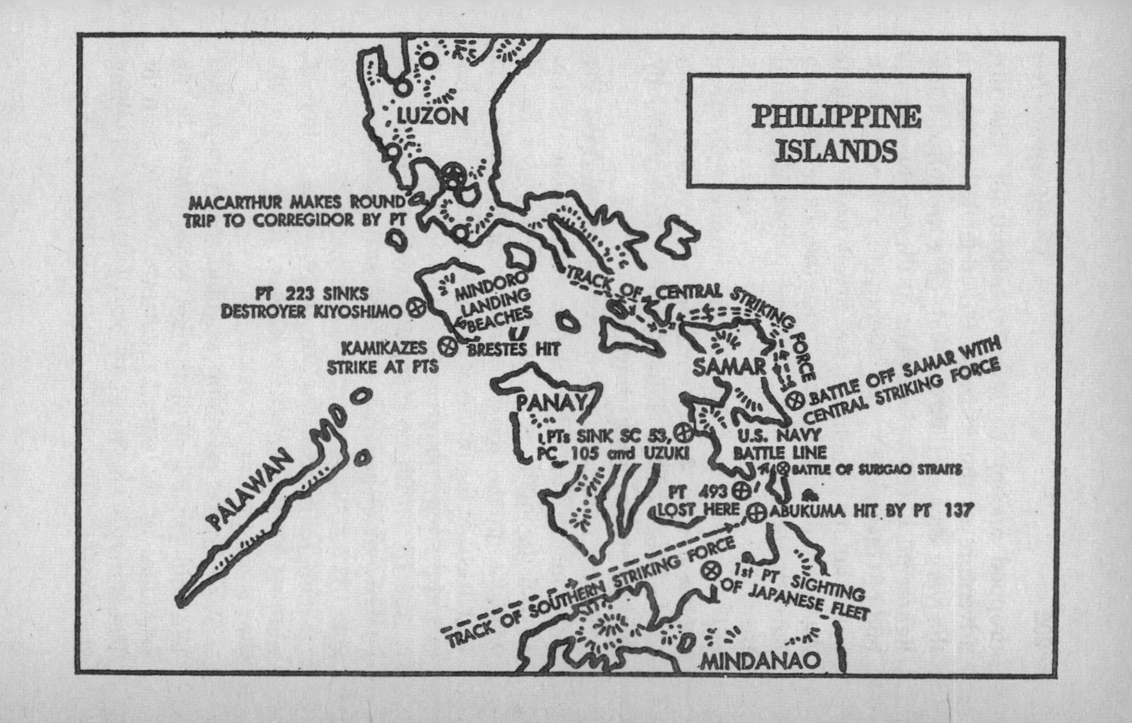
PHILIPPINE ISLANDS
LUZON
MACARTHUR MAKES ROUND TRIP TO CORREGIDOR BY PT
PT 223 SINKS DESTROYER KIYOSHIMO
MINDORO LANDING BEACHES
KAMIKAZES STRIKE AT PTS
BRESTES HIT
TRACK OF CENTRAL STRIKING FORCE
SAMAR
BATTLE OFF SAMAR WITH CENTRAL STRIKING FORCE
PANAY
LPTs SINK SC 53, PC 105 and UZUKI
U.S. NAVY BATTLE LINE
BATTLE OF SURIGAO STRAITS
PT 493 LOST HERE
ABUKUMA HIT BY PT 137
PALAWAN
TRACK OF SOUTHERN STRIKING FORCE
1st PT SIGHTING OF JAPANESE FLEET
MINDANAO

To make a coordinated attack, the two PTs hardly needed to communicate. They had gone through the motions so many times that they performed the maneuver like a reflex. The drill was to close a radar target slowly and silently to 200 yards, fire a mortar flare, and open fire with every gun that would bear instantly as the flare burst to smother the surprised Japanese before they could answer.

That split-second timing, the business of opening fire simultaneously with the bursting of the starshell, was drilled into gunners repeatedly by dummy attacks on floating logs.

Twenty-five miles short of the patrol area, the radar man found a target five miles off the beach. The two skippers were jubilant; here was a target made to order — too far out to sea to run for the beach, out of the range of protecting shore batteries, in water deep enough for a high-speed strafing run by the PTs, with no chance of hitting a rock. The boats went to general quarters and closed the target.

Lieut. Jones took the unnecessary precaution of warning his gunners. "Look alive, now — open fire the *instant* the flare goes off."

At 200 yards the skippers could make out a dim shape, but details of the target were hidden in the darkness. Lieut. Jones gave a last warning to gunners to be quick on the trigger, and fired his flare. Twenty-four gun barrels swung to bear on target.

The flare burst.

Lieut. Jones continues:

"There was the perfect target, a Jap barge loaded with troops – you could see their heads sticking up over the gunwale.

"*Open fire! Open fire!* I screamed in my mind, but no words came out of my mouth.

"What was the matter? Why weren't the guns firing? Thousands of tracers should be pouring into that enemy craft, but no gun on either PT fired. The flare died and I ordered another.

"Why was I doing this? Why wasn't the barge sinking now, holed by hundreds of shells? Why hadn't the gunners opened fire as ordered when the flare went off? And what was the matter on the Jap barge? Why weren't they tearing us up with their guns, for the flare lit us up as brightly as it illuminated them?

"We closed to 75 yards, still frozen in that strange paralysis under the glare of the dying starshell.

"My helmsman spoke up. 'They're not Japs, sir, they're natives.'

"I flipped on the searchlight, and our two boats circled the canoe, searchlights blazing, guns trained. That eerie scene will remain in my memory as long as I live. Thirty natives – some of them boys – sat rigidly still, staring forward unblinkingly. I don't know if it was native discipline or sheer terror that held them. Even the children didn't blink an eye or twitch a finger.

"We shouted to them that we were Americans, but we gave up trying to get through to them, for they refused to answer or even to turn their heads and look at us. We left them rigidly motionless and staring straight ahead at nothing.

"Back at the base we discussed our strange paralysis. Everybody agreed he had first thought it was a Jap barge when the flare burst, and nobody could give a reason for not shooting instantly. If even one gunner had fired, the whole weight of our broadside would have come down on that canoe.

"We'll never understand it, but we are all grateful to Whoever or Whatever it was that held our hands that night and spared those poor natives. And what woolly stories those Halmaherans must be telling their children about that night. I'll bet by now we are part of the sacred tribal legends of the whole Moluccan Archipelago."

Almost from the beginning of the return trip to the Philippines two years before, General MacArthur had had his eye on Mindanao, the southernmost large island of the group and hence the closest to Morotai. It was on Mindanao that he planned to land first, and from there he could advance up the island chain.

Before daring to venture into the Philippines, however, the Allied High Command wanted to make more landings — one at Yap Island, northeast of Palau (where Marines had landed the same day as the Morotai invasion), and another at Talaud Island, another steppingstone, about halfway between Morotai and Mindanao.

While the Palau and Morotai landings were going on – indeed a few days before they started, but too late to stop them – Admiral Halsey made a bold proposal to cancel all intermediate landings and take the biggest jump of all, completely over Talaud, over Yap, even over Mindanao itself, all the way to Leyte in the Central Philippines.

The Joint Chiefs of Staff of all the Allies, then at a conference in Quebec, swiftly accepted the recommendation and set October 20th as target date, chopping two months (and nobody will ever know how many casualties) off the life of the Pacific war.

In a wild flurry of activity, planners concentrated the preparations of three months into a month, diverted the forces for the other landings into Leyte force, and made bold carrier strikes at Formosa, in preparation for the landings in the Central Philippines.

An example of the incurable tendency of high-level Japanese officers to believe in their own foolish propaganda is the fact that on the very eve of the Leyte landings the Japanese defenders of the Philippines relaxed their guard, because they thought the Third Fleet had been wiped out.

American carriers had been roving the waters off Formosa during the week before the landings, and carrier planes had chewed up enemy airpower. Japanese Intelligence officers, however, believed the fantasies told them by their pilots returning from attacks on the American fleet. Radio Tokyo solemnly announced that the Third Fleet had been annihilated with the loss of 11 carriers, two battleships, three cruisers, and one destroyer.

The Japanese public went wild with enthusiasm. The Emperor made a special announcement of felicitation to his people, and victory celebrations were held at army and navy headquarters in the Philippines.

The Third Fleet had actually suffered two cruisers damaged.

The first American troops — a scouting force — landed on October 17th on Dinegat and Suluan islands, across the gulf from Leyte. Minesweepers swept the gulf and frogmen poked about the shoreline. Bombardment ships pounded the beaches, and carrier planes blasted enemy airfields. Ships of the attack landing forces entered Leyte Gulf during the night of October 19th, and next morning troops went ashore on four beaches on the west side of Leyte Gulf and on both sides of Panoan Strait, to the south.

PTs were rushed up from New Guinea, 1,200 miles away. Forty-five of the boats, under the tactical command of Lieut. Commander Robert Leeson, made the trip on their own power with a stopover for rest of a sort in Palau and a refueling at sea, so as to arrive with enough gas to start patrols immediately. They arrived in the combat zone on the morning of October 21st, and began prowling that same night.

Times were lively in Surigao Strait, and the PTs had good hunting, but nothing compared to what was coming.

Since a series of stinging setbacks from America's carrier planes during operations in the Central Pacific, the main body of the Japanese fleet – still a formidable host – had held back from fighting American ships in strength. Landings in the Philippines were too much to put up with, however – too close to the beloved homeland; His Imperial Japanese Majesty's ships had to fight now, no matter how desperate the situation – or rather because the situation *was* so desperate.

The Japanese executed a plan long held in readiness for just this event – the *Sho* plan, or Plan of Victory, as it was hopefully called, though the Japanese navy's chief of staff more realistically called it "Our last line of home defense."

The stage was set for the greatest naval battle of all time, the Battle of Leyte Gulf.

The naval lineup on the eve of battle – greatly simplified, perhaps oversimplified – was as follows:

U. S. Navy

Seventh Fleet, under Vice-Admiral Thomas Kincaid:

This slow but powerful force included six over-age battleships, 18 small, slow escort carriers, five heavy cruisers, six light cruisers, 86 destroyers, 25 destroyer escorts, 11 frigates, and the usual gunboats, supply train and landing craft for an amphibious operation – plus all the PTs on the scene, the 45 veterans of the New Guinea blockade. Mission of the Seventh Fleet was close support of the Sixth Army landing force.

Third Fleet, under Admiral William Halsey:

This fast and mighty force had six new fast battleships, 16 fast carriers, six heavy cruisers, nine light cruisers and 58 destroyers. Mission of the Third Fleet was to prowl the waters north of the landings on the lookout for a chance to destroy once and for all the main Japanese battle fleet, especially its remaining carriers.

Japanese Navy

Northern Decoy Force, under Vice-Admiral Ozawa:

Four fat carriers, prime targets for the aggressive Halsey, were screened by eight destroyers and one light cruiser. Mission of the force was suicidal. Without enough planes to make a serious fight, Admiral Ozawa nevertheless hoped to lure Halsey's powerful Third Fleet away from the landing beach, thus exposing American transports to attack by two powerful Japanese surface striking forces that were to sneak into Leyte Gulf through the back door, or rather two back doors at San Bernardino and Surigao Straits, north and south of Leyte Island.

Central Striking Force, under Vice-Admiral Kurita:

Five battleships, ten heavy cruisers, two light cruisers and 15 destroyers. Admiral Kurita was to take this formidable surface fleet through San Bernardino Straits, at the northern tip of Samar, to come down on the transports "like a wolf on the fold" while Halsey's force was wasting time on the sacrificial carrier decoy in the north.

Southern Striking Force, under Vice-Admiral Shima:

Formed of two task units—a vanguard under Admiral Nishima of two battleships, one heavy cruiser and four destroyers, plus a second section under Admiral Shima of two heavy cruisers, one light cruiser and four destroyers. These two southern forces were to come up from the East Indies and pass through Surigao Straits —happy hunting grounds of the PTs—to join with the Central Striking Force in Leyte Gulf for the unopposed and leisurely destruction of the Sixth Army.

The Japanese apparently could not believe that the U.S. Navy — once Halsey had been suckered into chasing off after the decoy carriers — had enough ships left afloat to resist the two striking forces. Had not the entire Japanese nation just celebrated an Imperial proclamation of the near annihilation of the American fleet?

All three Japanese forces converged on the Philippines simultaneously. By October 24th, the three forces had been spotted and reported by Allied scouts. Torpedoes and bombs from planes and submarines had made punishing hits on the advancing Central and Southern Striking Forces, but the ships kept plodding on toward the straits north and south of Leyte.

And Admiral Halsey snapped at the bait dangled by Admiral Ozuma's carriers. For a man of Admiral Halsey's temperament, the reported sighting of the northern carrier group was too much to resist. He lit out to get them all—leaving unguarded the Strait of San Bernardino, back gate into Leyte Gulf and the transport area.

For once, an American command staff had fallen into the chronic error of the Japanese. Admiral Halsey apparently believed the exaggerated claims of his pilots and thought that the Central Striking Force had been decimated and the remnants driven off. The Japanese had actually lost only three cruisers to submarines and a battleship to aircraft. After a short retreat, Admiral Kurita reconsidered and turned back during the night to resume the transit of San Bernardino Strait. His powerful fleet was steaming toward the transport area at 20 knots.

Admiral Kincaid misinterpreted a message from Admiral Halsey and thought a part of his Third Fleet was still on station, corking up San Bernardino, so Kincaid dismissed the central force from his mind and turned his attention to the southern force heading for Surigao Strait. Not even a scout submarine was watching the northern pass into Leyte Gulf.

Shortly after noon of October 24th, Admiral Kincaid notified his entire command to prepare for a battle that night. He cleared Surigao Strait of all unnecessary traffic, and gave Rear Admiral Jesse Oldendorf the job of not only stopping but destroying the enemy column.

Admiral Oldendorf had been commanding the

bombardment and support forces, and had in his control all the heavy guns of the Seventh Fleet. In a phrase which infuriated the Japanese when they heard it, Oldendorf said that he deployed his forces according to the professional gambler's code: "Never give a sucker a chance."

Surigao Strait is a narrow strip of water about thirty-five miles long, running almost north-south between Leyte and Dinegat islands. By its shape and location, the strait was going to force the Southern Striking Force to approach Leyte Gulf in a long, narrow column. Admiral Oldendorf deployed his ancient but still hard-punching battleships in a line across the mouth of the strait where it opens into Leyte Gulf. Thus, without further maneuver, Oldendorf was certain to open fire with his battle line already crossing the T of the Japanese column. His fleet could swing its entire broadside to bear simultaneously; the enemy could fire only the forward turrets on the lead ship.

Admiral Oldendorf was not satisfied with depending entirely on this setup, murderous as it was, so he deployed every other fighting ship in his command to work maximum destruction on the Japanese. He posted cruisers and destroyers between the battleships and the mouth of the straits, as a combined screen and supplementary battle line. Other destroyer squadrons were posted near the strait, so that they could launch torpedoes and then get out of the way during the gunfire phase of the battle.

Admiral Oldendorf's position was good — except for one thing. The warships had fired off most of their ammunition in beach bombardment, and magazine stocks were low, especially in the armor-piercing shells needed for fighting heavy battleships. Oldendorf ordered the battleships to hold their fire until they were sure of making hits — and he ordered maximum use of torpedoes.

That meant torpedo boats, so 39 of Commander Selman Bowling's PTs were deployed in 13 sections of three boats each along the shores of Surigao Strait, and also along the coasts of Mindanao and Bohol islands, far into the Mindanao Sea on the other end of Surigao Strait. The farthest PTs were stationed 100 miles from the battleline.

The Seventh Fleet had no night scouting planes, so Admiral Oldendorf informed the PTs that their primary mission was scouting. The boats were to patrol the approaches to the strait and to hide along the wooded shores fringing the coming scene of battle. They were to relay radio contact reports as the Japanese passed their station.

Then they were to attack and do all the torpedo damage possible before the Japanese came within gunshot of the Seventh Fleet battleline.

The PTs took up their stations during the night, and all hands topside peered out to sea, watching for the telltale white bow wave of the first Japanese ship.

The torpedo boat actions that followed are often hard to understand. PTs, by the nature of their attack, provoke wild melees, and survivors of melees rarely remember precisely what happened. What they do claim to remember is usually faulty and contradicted by circumstantial evidence. PT skippers kept only sketchy logs, and those entries giving the time an action took place are often especially inaccurate. As nearly as a historian can tell, however, here is what happened to the PTs.

At 10:15 P.M. Ensign Peter R. Gadd, skipper of PT 131, on station 18 miles south of Bohol Island almost exactly in the middle of the Mindanao Sea and 100 miles from Admiral Oldendorf, picked up two targets on his radar screen. They were between the three-boat section commanded by Lieut. W. C. Pullen, and Bohol Island to the north. Lieut. Pullen tried to reach Admiral Oldendorf by radio, but failed, so he led the PTs 152, 130 and 131, in a torpedo approach.

The radar pips broke into five separate targets, and when a light haze lifted, the skippers clearly saw what they thought were two battleships, two cruisers and a destroyer. The enemy opened fire at three-mile range, with his biggest batteries. Starshells burst overhead and the PTs tore away through a ghastly glare that made them feel naked under the rain of high explosive.

An eight-inch shell hit a torpedo of 130 smack on the warhead and tore through the bow. Miraculously, there was no explosion.

The 152 was hit by a 4.7-incher, probably from a destroyer that was closing fast, with searchlight blazing. (This destroyer, the *Shigure*, was the only ship of the Japanese van to survive the coming massacre.) The explosion tore away the 37-mm. cannon, killed the gunner, stunned the loader, and wounded three sailors. The boat was afire.

Aboard the stricken 152, Lieut. (jg) Joseph Eddins dumped two shallow-set depth charges into his wake and pumped 40-mm. shells at the pursuing destroyer.

"Our 40 mm. made the enemy reluctant to continue the use of the searchlight," said Lieut Eddins.

The destroyer snapped off the light and sheered away from the geysers of exploding depth charges.

The fight had lasted 23 minutes. Now there were two more targets on the radar screen and the PT sailors were frantic to get their radio report through to the waiting battleline.

Lieut. (jg) Ian D. Malcolm of 130 ran south until he found Lieut. (jg) John A. Cady's section near Camiguin Island. He boarded PT 127 and borrowed its radio. Just after midnight on October 25th, Lieut. Malcolm made the first contact report of the position, course, and speed of the enemy. It was the first word of the enemy received by Admiral Oldendorf in fourteen hours.

Aboard the 152, the crew put out the fire, and the skipper gave the boat a little test run. The bow was stove in, but the plucky boat could still make 24 knots, so Lieut. Pullen ordered a stern chase of the disappearing Japanese. He had to abandon the attack, however, because the Japanese were too fast for him to catch. There is something touching and ludicrous in the picture of the tiny, bashed-up PT trying to catch the mammoth Japanese battleline.

Lieut. (jg) Dwight H. Owen, in charge of a section near Limasawa Island next picked up signs of the approaching fleet. He tells how it looked:

"The prologue began just before midnight. Off to the southwest over the horizon we saw distant flashes of gunfire, starshells bursting and far-off sweep of searchlights. The display continued about fifteen minutes, then blacked out. Squalls came and went. One moment the moon shone bright as day, and the next you couldn't make out the bow of your boat. Then the radar developed the sort of pips you read about."

Lieut. Owen jumped for the radio, but the enemy was jamming the circuit and he could not get his report off. He did the next best thing—he attacked.

At 1,800 yards, the cruiser *Mogami* snapped on its searchlight and probed for the boats. PT 146 (Ensign B. M. Grosscup), and 150 (Ensign J. M.

Ladd), fired one fish each, but missed. The destroyer *Yumagumo* caught the 151 and the 190 in a searchlight beam, but the boats raked the destroyer with 40-mm. fire and knocked out the lights. The boats zigzagged away behind smoke.

Admiral Nishimura, commanding this van force of the two-section Southern Striking Force, was delighted with himself at this point, and sent a message to Admiral Shima, congratulating himself on having sunk several torpedo boats.

At the southern entrance to Surigao Strait, Lieut. Commander Robert Leeson, on PT 134, commanded the section posted on the western shore. The boat crews saw flashes of the battle with Lieut. Owen's boats, and half an hour later picked up radar pips ten miles away. Leeson promptly passed the radar sighting to Admiral Oldendorf, and then – the milder duty done – led a torpedo attack.

Lieut. (jg) Edmund F. Wakelin's 134 was caught by a searchlight while still 3,000 yards from the two battleships. Shells fell close aboard on both sides, splashing water over the boat, and shrapnel from air bursts banged against the deck, but the skipper bore in another 500 yards to launch his fish. The boat escaped from the Japanese and hid in the shadow of Panaon Island, where later in the night the sailors fumed helplessly as four Japanese ships steamed, "fat, dumb, and happy," past their empty torpedo tubes at 1,000-yard range.

All the torpedo tubes of the section were not empty, however, for Lieut. (jg) I. M. Kovar, in 137, at 3:55 A.M., picked up an enemy formation at the southern end of the strait and attacked. He had no way of knowing it, but this was Admiral Shima's second section, coming up to the relief of Admiral Nishimura's van that had already entered the strait, and indeed had at that very moment been shattered by a vicious American destroyer-torpedo attack.

Lieut. Kovar crept up on a Japanese destroyer, maneuvering to take station at the rear of the enemy column. He let fly at the can and had the incredible good luck to miss his target entirely and smack a light cruiser he hadn't even seen. Aboard the cruiser *Abukuma*, the explosion killed thirty sailors, destroyed the radio shack and slowed the cruiser to ten knots, forcing it to fall out of formation.

The crippled *Abukuma* was caught and polished off by Army bombers the next day. It was the only victim of Army aviation in this battle and the only positively verified victim of PT torpedoes, though there is some evidence that a PT may have made one of the hits claimed by American destroyers.

The rest of Admiral Shima's formation sailed majestically up the strait, fired a spread of torpedoes at two small islands it mistook for American warships, and managed somehow to collide with the fiercely burning cruiser *Mogami*, only survivor — except for the destroyer *Shigure* — of the vanguard's slaughter by the torpedoes and guns of the Seventh Fleet.

Gathering in the two surviving ships, Admiral Shima led a retreat down the strait. At the moment *Shigure* joined the formation, Lieut. C. T. Gleason's section attacked, and the Japanese destroyer, which was doing some remarkably able shooting, hit Ensign L. E. Thomas' 321.

Most sorely hit of the torpedo boats, however, was Lieut. (jg) R. W. Brown's 493, which had had John F. Kennedy aboard, as an instructor, for a month in Miami. The crew had named the boat the *Carole Baby* after the skipper's daughter, who, incidentally, was celebrating her first birthday the night of the Battle of Surigao Strait.

Lieut. Brown tells the *Carole Baby's* story:

"I was assigned a division of boats to take position directly down the middle of the strait between Panaon and Dinegat.

"While we were under way to take station, the moon was out but heavy overcast on the horizon threatened to bring complete darkness later. We spotted an occasional light on the beach and we passed an occasional native sailing craft, so the crew's light mood changed to tension, because they thought we were being spied on.

"When we were on station, strung out across the channel so that the Japs couldn't get by without our seeing them, I stretched out on the dayroom deck for a little relaxation, but the radio crackled the report that the first PT patrols had made contact.

"'All hands to General Quarters,' I ordered. 'Take echelon formation and prepare to attack.'

"The radarman called up 'Skipper, eight targets distant twelve miles, estimated speed 28 knots.'

"We closed to three miles, and seconds later my number two boat reported its four torpedoes were in the water. Number Three reported two more fish off and running. I had been maneuvered out of firing position and hadn't launched any torpedoes yet, so I came around for another attack and was separated from the rest of the section.

"Powerful searchlights pinpointed the two other boats, and starshells lit up the night with their ugly green glare. The two other boats shot up the enemy can and knocked out two of the lights. I didn't open fire, because the Japs hadn't seen the *Carole Baby* yet and I wanted to shoot my fish before they found me.

"At about 500 yards, I fired two and opened up with my guns. The enemy fired starshells and turned on the searchlights. At this close range we could see Japanese sailors scrambling about the ship, and we poured it into them, but the concussion of their exploding shells was creeping steadily closer, so I ordered my executive officer, Nick Carter, to come hard left, open the throttles and GET OUT!

"I went aft to release smoke for a screen so we

could return to fire our remaining torpedoes, but we had penetrated an outer destroyer screen without knowing it and had Japs all around us. Eight searchlights pinned us down like a bug on a needle.

"It's a funny thing how the mind works. I took time at that moment to notice that all those searchlights were turning the sea about us to a beautiful phosphorescent green.

"Our guns blew up two of the searchlights, but we were being hit hard. A. W. Brunelle reported from the engine room that the boat was badly holed at the waterline. I found out later that he took off his kapok life jacket and stuffed it into the hole as the only cork he could find right at hand.

"A blinding flash and terrific concussion threw me out of the cockpit. Stunned, I reeled forward to find that most of the chartroom had been blown away.

"I told Nick to head the *Carole Baby* for the Island of Panaon, and we limped off with the Jap cans chasing us. When we were out of torpedo range of the capital ships, they turned back but kept throwing shells at us to be sure we didn't return to attack.

"*Return to attack!* We weren't even sure we could stay afloat. The engines were almost completely underwater and though they were still working, they couldn't chug along forever with water steadily rising in the hold.

"The last destroyer left us just as the bow of the *Carole Baby* scraped on a coral reef one hundred yards off the beach at Panaon.

"When the shooting stopped, a weird silence settled over us. I went over the boat to see what condition we were in. We were in bad condition. The *Carole Baby* had been hit by five shells. Two of them had passed clean through us without exploding, but the one that had exploded in the charthouse had killed two and wounded nine of my crew.

"And that isn't all. We were high on a reef, within rock-throwing distance of an enemy shore. I had to know if those lights we could see came from a Japanese camp, so I armed ten of us with machine guns and grenades and we slipped over the side.

"We found a little village. Somebody had been there, but had run off as we approached, so we decided to search farther. This type of warfare was different from the one the crew was used to, and everybody was ill at ease."

It is interesting to note that by inference the sailors were *not* "ill at ease" in the type of warfare they had just been subjected to.

"One of the sailors was almost strangled by what he thought was a low-hanging vine, but we found it was a telephone wire leading to a small hut. We crept close to the hut and listened. No good. Japanese!

"We cut the wire and returned to the safety of our reef."

Again, consider the character of sailors who talk about the "safety" of a shattered boat, filled with dead and wounded shipmates, stranded on a rock in the midst of history's greatest naval battle and within pistol range of an enemy shore.

"We expected that wire-cutting bit would stir up some Jap patrols, so we made ourselves into a Little Gibraltar with all the weapons we could scrape together – and on a PT boat that is plenty of weapons."

Lieut. Brown tells of settling down to enjoy the unaccustomed role of spectator at a battle. Through the night the crew watched the flash and glare of gunfire and exploding ships up the straits.

"We couldn't tell who was faring best. Through binoculars we could see ships afire and sinking, but we couldn't tell if they were Japanese or American. Long before dawn the eastern sky looked like sunrise, because of the orange glow of burning ships.

"When day did break we saw natives creeping back to their village, so we waved and yelled '*Americanos*' and '*Amigos*' and friendly stuff like that. They finally believed us and waded out to our boat where the sailors set about their eternal bargaining for souvenirs. I believe an American sailor would bargain with a cannibal tribe while they're putting him into the pot.

"One of the crew yelled and pointed out to sea. Three PTs were roaring up the straits in broad daylight and we could see what they were after – it was the crippled cruiser *Mogami,* trying to limp home after the fight.

"I watched one of the PTs fire two fish and then race toward us when the cruiser fired at her. We were glad to see her coming, but then we realized with horror that the skipper thought our poor beat-up old *Carole Baby* was a Japanese barge, and he was getting ready to make a strafing run on us. We jumped up and down and waved our arms and yelled like crazy, even though we knew they couldn't hear us.

"Just before they got to the spot where I would have opened fire if I had been skipper, we saw the gunners relax and point those gun muzzles away as they recognized us. It was PT 491 that came to our rescue.

"We tried to pull the *Carole Baby* off the reef, but she was too far gone. She went down in deep water – the only American ship, incidentally, lost in the Battle of Surigao Strait."

Admiral Chester W. Nimitz radioed from Hawaii:

THE SKILL, DETERMINATION AND COURAGE DISPLAYED BY THE PERSONNEL OF THESE SMALL BOATS IS WORTHY OF THE HIGHEST PRAISE. . . . THE PT ACTION VERY PROBABLY THREW THE JAPANESE

COMMAND OFF BALANCE AND CONTRIBUTED TO THE COMPLETENESS OF THEIR SUBSEQUENT DEFEAT.

By contrast to the corking of Surigao Strait, at the unguarded San Bernardino Strait, the powerful Central Striking Force that morning passed unopposed into Leyte Gulf and jumped the escort carriers and their screen. Something close to world-wide panic broke out in American command centers when the brass realized that the Central Striking Force was already in the gulf and Admiral Halsey's force was off chasing the carrier decoy – too far off to engage Kurita's fleet.

A handful of destroyers and destroyer escorts of the screen threw themselves between the Japanese wolf and the transport sheep. Planes from the escort carriers made real and dummy bombing runs on Kurita's ships. Between them the desperate escort forces – planes and destroyers – battled Kurita to a standstill in the most spectacular show of sheer fighting courage in all of naval history.

Incredibly, Admiral Kurita, with a victory as great as Pearl Harbor within his grasp – the very victory that the northern decoy carrier force was being sacrificed to buy – turned his mighty fleet about and steamed back through San Bernardino Strait, content with sinking two of the escort carriers and three of the screen ships whose gallant skippers had put their destroyers between the enemy and the helpless transport fleet.

Admiral Halsey sank all four carriers, three destroyers, one light cruiser and a fleet oiler of the decoy force.

The *Sho* plan had worked almost perfectly for the Japanese — but with an unexpected outcome; the Japanese surface fleet, instead of wiping out the American transport fleet, was shattered. Its carrier force virtually vanished. His Imperial Japanese Majesty's navy could never mount a major attack again.

With the main battleline of the Japanese fleet driven from the scene, the PTs were right back where they had been in New Guinea and Guadalcanal — busting barges and derailing the Tokyo Express.

On the far side of Leyte Island the waters are reef filled, the channels shallow and tortuous. The Japanese were using the dangerous waters of the Camotes Sea and Ormoc Bay to land supplies at night behind their lines. A familiar enough situation for the PT sailors, so the skippers took their shallow-draft torpedo boats into Ormoc Bay, looking for trouble.

On the night between November 28th and 29th, Lieut. Roger H. Hallowell took PTs 127, 331, 128, and 191 around the tip of Leyte and headed up the western shore for Ormoc Bay in the first combat patrol of those waters.

PTs 127 and 331 entered the bay while the other two boats patrolled the islands outside. In the light of a tropical moon, the skippers inside saw a subchaser and crept to within 800 yards before the Japanese opened fire. The two boats launched eight torpedoes and a ripple of rockets (enough explosive to tear a battleship in two, much less a little patrol craft). The retiring PT skippers reported the usual loud explosion, indicating a torpedo hit, which virtually all retiring torpedo-boat captains always reported. This time, however, they were right. The Japanese themselves later admitted the loss of the subchaser SC 53.

The two retiring boats, all their torpedoes spent, met the 128 and 191 at the entrance to the bay, and Lieut. Hallowell "transferred his flag" to the 128 to lead the two still-armed boats in a second attack.

All four boats went in, the two boats with spent tubes planning to give gunfire support to the armed duo. All hands searched for the original target, but could not find it – for the good reason that it was on the bottom.

Lieut. Hallowell saw what he thought was a freighter tied to a dock, so the two skippers, ignoring fire from the beach, launched all torpedoes.

Ten days later, when the Army had landed at Ormoc and taken over the harbor, the PTs promptly moved in and discovered that Lieut. Hallowell's "freighter" was the Japanese PC 105, clearly visible at the dock, sitting on the bottom with a fatal gash in her side.

Lieut. Melvin W. Haines, early on the morning of December 12th, led PTs 492 and 490 in a classic attack on a convoy in Ormoc Bay. The PTs stalked silently to close range, launched torpedoes, and retired zigzagging behind smoke in a maneuver right out of the PT textbook. They were rewarded by a great stab of light behind them. One of the boats, or perhaps both, had hit the destroyer *Uzuki*, which went up in a great column of orange flame.

This kind of night warfare was only too tediously familiar to PT sailors, but right then the war took a nasty new turn for them – indeed for the whole Pacific Fleet.

Desperate because of the swift deterioration of their position, the Japanese switched from all reasonable kinds of warfare – if there are such – and developed the suicidal *kamikaze* tactic.

Through the war, Japanese fliers – and Americans, too, for that matter – already hit and doomed, often tried to crash-land on ships under attack, to take the enemy down to death with them.

During the Leyte surface-air battles, however, many of the Japanese were dedicated, with great ceremony, to making deliberate suicide dives into

American ships, as a kind of human bomb. The toll was already frightening to American naval men, and threatened to get worse.

In mid-December two *kamikaze* planes crashed into the 323 in Surigao Strait, and destroyed it utterly so that the PTs crews were served notice that they were not too small a prize to merit attention from the sinister new air fleet.

MacArthur had returned, all right, when he went ashore at Leyte, but it was only a kind of tentative return – a one-foot-in-the-door return. Until he landed on Corregidor in Luzon, he wouldn't really be back where he started. Luzon was the goal.

Just across the narrow Verde Island Passage from Luzon is the island of Mindoro, and MacArthur's air commanders sorely coveted that piece of real estate for airstrips so that they could bring Luzon under the gunsights of their fighters before the Luzon landings began.

On December 12th MTB Squadrons Thirteen and Sixteen, plus PTs 227 and 230, left Leyte Gulf in a convoy with the Eighth Army's Visayan Task Force to invade Mindoro Bay, 300 miles to the northwest. Because of the sharply mounting *kamikaze* attacks, the Navy did not want to risk a tender in Mindoro waters, so the squadrons, with the help of the ingenious Seabees, planned to set up a base of sorts on an LST.

During the afternoon of December 13th, a *kamikaze* slipped through the air cover and crashed into the portside of the invasion force flagship, the cruiser *Nashville.* The pilot carried two bombs, and their explosion touched off five-inch and 40-mm. ammunition in the ready lockers topside. The shattering blast killed 133 officers and men, including both the Army and Navy chiefs of staff and the colonel commanding the bombardment wing. The *Nashville* had to return to Leyte Gulf.

Later, ten more Japanese planes attacked and one got through to the destroyer *Haraden.* The explosion killed 14 sailors and the destroyer had to go back to Leyte. The PTs huddled close to the rest of the convoy, to add their batteries to the curtain of fire.

Troops went ashore on Mindoro at 7 A.M. on December 15th, and met little opposition. Half an hour later, PTs were operating in the harbor. The infantry quickly set up a perimeter defense, pushing back the small Japanese garrison to make room for an airfield at San Jose. As they had at Bougainville, American planners wanted only enough room on Mindoro to establish and protect a fighter base. It was not Mindoro but Luzon that was the basic goal.

The Japanese didn't intend to let the Americans have even that much land, however, without lashing back furiously at the invaders of this island almost within sight of the city of Manila.

Just after 8 A.M. the *kamikazes* arrived. Three of the planes dove on destroyers and were shot down by the combined fire of all ships. The fourth flew over the stern of Ensign J. P. Rafferty's PT 221, caught the full blast of the PT battery, and cartwheeled along the surface of the bay, spraying water and flames until it sank from sight.

Outside the bay, the sailors saw the *kamikazes* coming, so Lieut. Commander Alvin W. Fargo, Jr., commanding Squadron Thirteen, ordered the PTs still escorting the convoy to get between the LSTs and the approaching planes. Seven *kamikazes* strafed the PTs ineffectively, and the boats brought down three of them. Of the four that penetrated the screen, two were shot down by the combined fire of the LSTs and the PTs. The other two dived into LST 472 and LST 738, setting them afire. Eventually, destroyers had to sink the burning hulks with gunfire. PTs picked up a hundred survivors.

Next morning all the PTs were in Mangarin Bay at Mindoro, site of the landings, and the LST 605, destined to be their base ship, was unloading on the beach. PTs 230 and 300 were entering from the night's patrol, when a single plane glided out of the sun and strafed the 230, without hitting it. The *kamikaze* circled and started his dive on the LST 605. The landing ship and all the PTs opened fire and shot off the plane's tail. The *kamikaze* crashed on the beach fifty yards from the LST, killing five men and wounding 11.

Half an hour later eight planes came after the PTs.

Lieut. (jg) Byron F. Kent, whose 230 was a target, tells of applying broken-field running football tactics to the problem:

"Three of the planes chose my boat as their target. All our fire was concentrated on the first as it dove for the boat in a gradual sweep, increasing to an angle of about seventy degrees. I maneuvered at high speed, to present a starboard broadside to the oncoming plane. When it was apparent that the plane could not pull out of the dive, I feinted in several directions and then turned hard right rudder under the plane. It struck the water thirty feet off the starboard bow.

"The second plane began its dive. When the pilot committed himself to his final direction, I swung the boat away from the plane's right bank. The plane hit the water fifty feet away.

"The third plane came in at a seventy-degree dive. After zigzagging rapidly as the plane came down, I swung suddenly at right angles. The plane landed in the water just astern, raising the stern out of the water and showering the 40-mm. gun crew with flame, smoke, debris, and water. All of us were slightly dazed, but there were no injuries and the boat was undamaged."

Lieut. (jg) Frank A. Tredinnick, in 77, was attacked by a single. He held a steady course and speed until just before impact, and then chopped his throttle. The *kamikaze* pilot, who had quite properly taken a lead on the speeding boat, crashed ten yards ahead.

Lieut. (jg) Harry Griffin, Jr. swung his 223 hard right just before impact, and his attacker showered the boat with water.

With two planes after him, Lieut. (jg) J. R. Erickson maneuvered at top speed.

"The gunners fired a steady stream of shells into one plane as it came down in a steep dive and crashed fifteen feet off the port bow. The second plane circled until he saw his partner had missed, and he dived on our stern, strafing as he came. The gunners fired on him until he crashed *three feet* off the starboard bow, spraying the deck with debris and water. One man was blown over the side by the concussion but was rescued uninjured."

The last plane was shot down by the combined fire of the PTs before it could even pick a target.

That afternoon as 224 and 297 were leaving for the night's patrol, two planes dropped three bombs but missed. The ships in the bay shot one plane into the water. The other was last seen gliding over the treetops, trailing fire.

On the afternoon of December 17th, three planes came into the bay. One went into a steep dive aimed at Lieut. Commander Almer P. Colvin's 300. The *kamikaze* had been studying the failure of his comrades, with their suicidal sacrifice, to inflict any damage on the swift PTs. Lieut. Commander

Colvin gave the 300 a last-second twist to the right, but the pilot outsmarted him, anticipated that very move, and crashed into the engine room, splitting the boat in two. The stern sank immediately and the bow burned for eight hours. Lieut. Commander Colvin was seriously wounded, four men were killed, four reported missing, one officer and four men wounded. Only one man aboard escaped without injury.

That night Lieut. Commander N. Burt Davis' boats carried sealed orders from General MacArthur to a guerrilla hideout on the other side of Mindoro and delivered them to Lieut. Commander George F. Rowe, U. S. Navy liaison officer to the Mindoro Underground. The boats picked up eleven American pilots, who had been rescued and sheltered by the guerrillas, and brought them back to Mindoro.

Some of the Japanese High Command wanted to write Mindoro off as already lost; others wanted to make a massive counterlanding on the north beaches to fight it out at the perimeter defense and push the American airfield off the island. The two groups compromised, and as often happens in a compromise, they sent a boy to do a man's job.

Admiral Kimura left Indo-China with a heavy cruiser, a light cruiser, and four destroyers, on a mission of bombarding the Mindoro beachhead. It wasn't much of a naval task force to send into those waters, but as it happens, every American capital ship in the area was at Leyte, too far off to help. The only naval forces handy were the PTs.

The PTs had been up against this very problem before. Twice, at Guadalcanal, they had tangled alone with a bombardment force and a far mightier bombardment force than the one approaching from Indo-China.

"Recall all patrols to assist in the defense of Mindoro," Lieut. Admiral Kincaid ordered Lieut. Commander Davis.

A patrol line of the nine most seaworthy boats was strung out three miles off the beach. Two more boats, under Lieut. P. A. Swart, had already left to call on the Mindoro guerrillas, but Davis called them back, vectoring them toward the approaching Japanese, with instructions to attack on contact.

Army bombers attacked the Japanese bombardment flotilla all night long (and attacked the patrolling PTs, too, seriously damaging 77 with a near miss and wounding every member of the crew – which was more than the *kamikazes* had been able to do in days of ferocious attack).

Admiral Kimura bombarded the beach for about thirty minutes. It was a most desultory job, did almost no damage, and caused not a single casualty. He fired three poorly aimed salvos at the PTs and left.

Halfway up the western coast of Mindoro, Admiral Kimura ran into Lieut. Swart's two PTs, hustling back to get into the scrap. Just after midnight the two boat skippers and the Japanese discovered each other simultaneously. The Japanese illuminated 220 with a searchlight and fired dangerously accurate salvos — the first good shooting that force had done that night.

Lieut. (jg) Harry Griffin, Jr., closed his 223 to 4,000 yards and fired both his starboard fish. Three minutes later a long lance of flame shot up from the ship's side and she went under the waves.

The next afternoon PTs picked up five Japanese sailors from the water. They were survivors of the brand new destroyer *Kiyoshimo,* victim of Lieut. Griffin's steady eye.

The worst ordeal of the Mindoro landings was prepared on December 27th, when a resupply convoy shaped up near Dulag on Leyte Island. The convoy led off with 25 LSTs in five columns of five ships; next came three Liberty ships, one Navy tanker, six Army tankers, two aviation gasoline tankers and the PT tender *Orestes* in five columns at the center of the convoy; last came 23 LCIs in five columns. Nine destroyers formed an outer screen; 29 PTs formed an inner screen on each flank.

Aboard the *Orestes* was Captain G. F. Mentz, commander of the Diversionary Attack Group of LCIs and PTs which was being moved to Mindoro for mounting amphibious landings behind the Japanese lines.

A Japanese night snooper spotted the convoy about 4 A.M. on December 28th, and at the same time the convoy commander learned that the weather was so bad over Leyte airfields that he could expect no air cover until noon the next day. Unfortunately the weather was fine over the convoy – perfect weather for the *kamikazes* to draw a bead on the slow ships of the supply train.

In midmorning three planes attacked. The first tried to crash-dive the LCIs and was shot down by LCI 1076. Another overshot the aviation gasoline tanker *Porcupine*, and splashed.

The third *kamikaze* made perhaps the most spectacular suicide crash of the war. It hit the *John Burke*, a merchant ship loaded with ammunition, and pilot, plane, ship, cargo, and crew disappeared in a blinding flash. A small Army freighter went down with the *John Burke*. The LCI flagship, LCI 624, ran to the rescue, but only two heads bobbed in the water, both survivors of the Army ship, and one of those died almost immediately. All sixty-eight merchant sailors had been vaporized in the explosion.

Another *kamikaze* hit the merchant ship *William Ahearne* on the bridge, setting it on fire. The ship was towed back to Leyte. Loss of this ship was a sad blow to the forces ashore at Mindoro, for included in her cargo was a large stock of beer.

Friendly air cover arrived and ran off that particular flight of planes, but the convoy was under almost constant attack that night. In the moonlight, about 7 P.M., a torpedo bomber put a fatal fish into LST 750.

Three LCIs each shot down a plane. Sailors on the LCI flagship had the harrowing experience of hearing a torpedo scrape along the ship's flat bottom from stem to stern without exploding. Some of the LCIs had surgical units aboard, and many of the wounded were run over to these handy, impromptu hospital ships.

Air attack was incessant, in daylight and dark, and too monotonously similar to recount in detail unless there was scoring.

During the morning of December 30th, three planes were shot down, one by a PT that knocked down its victim as the *kamikaze* was diving on an escorting destroyer.

The last attack of the morning came just as the convoy was entering the harbor at San Jose. The landing-craft flagship shot down a *kamikaze* with a short burst of 40 mm.

Inside Mangarin Bay the ships hurried with the stevedoring, because the sailors were eager to leave this unfriendly land. No planes appeared until almost 4 P.M.

Five Japanese dive-bombers pierced the friendly fighter cover and whistled down from 14,000 feet in their suicide dives. One hit the destroyer *Pringle* and did only light damage. Another hit the aviation gasoline tanker *Porcupine* with such an impact that its engine went clear through the decks and out the bottom, tearing a large hole in the hull. Seven men were killed and eight wounded. The stern burst into flames, a dangerous development on a ship carrying a tankful of aviation gasoline forward.

The fourth plane dove on the destroyer *Gansevoort* and crashed it amidships. The main deck was peeled back like the lid of an empty sardine can. The impact cut power lines and set fires, but caused surprisingly light casualties.

The destroyer *Wilson* came alongside and exercised the fire-fighting crew by putting them aboard the *Gansevoort* to fight the flames.

The *Gansevoort* was towed to the PT base. There she was given the bizarre task of torpedoing the burning *Porcupine* to knock off the blazing stern before the fire reached the gasoline tanks forward. The trick didn't work, for the blast just spread burning gasoline on the water, endangering the *Gansevoort* herself and setting new fires, so she had to be towed to a new anchorage. There she was abandoned, but a volunteer crew of a nearby PT boarded the destroyer and put out the fires. *Porcupine* burned to the waterline.

The most grievous blow of the *kamikaze* attack, however, was struck at the PT navy.

The fifth Japanese dive bomber dove on the PT tender *Orestes,* was hit by tracers from PTs and LCIs, hit the water and bounced upward into the starboard side of the tender. The plane's bombs punched through the side and exploded within, blowing many officers and men into the bay. The ship burst into violent flame, and fire mains were ruptured by the blast. Fifty-nine men were killed and 106 seriously wounded.

The waters around the *Orestes* were teeming with swimming sailors, and PTs bustled about, pulling in the stunned survivors of the blast.

The LCI 624 went alongside and Commander A. V. Jannotta, the LCI flotilla commander, led a volunteer fire-fighting and rescue party aboard the ship, which had become a hell of exploding ammunition and burning aviation gasoline.

Commander Jannotta was awarded a Navy Cross for his heroic salvage work of that afternoon. Captain Mentz had been severely wounded in the *kamikaze* blast, and his chief of staff, Commander John Kremer, Jr., had been killed, so Commander Jannotta took over as commander of the whole task group. He was given a Silver Star for his performance in that capacity.

Led by Lieut. Commander Davis, many PT sailors went aboard the burning *Orestes* to pull wounded shipmates out of the fire.

By 9:45 P.M., flames were out on the *Orestes* and Commander Jannotta lashed an LCI to either side and pushed it up on the beach.

At dusk, PTs and LCIs scattered and hugged

the shoreline, to make the worst possible targets for night marauders. The small craft had good reason to be shaken. The five *kamikazes* had made 100 per cent hits, and any weapon that is 100 per cent effective is a fearsome weapon.

That same night four PTs shot down a plane as they left the bay on patrol.

Early in the morning of New Year's Day, 1945, bombers came over the base again. One fragmentation bomb killed 11 men and seriously wounded ten others, most of them survivors of the *Orestes*.

The *kamikazes* were not through with the Mindoro shipping. On the afternoon of January 4th, PTs 78 and 81 set fire to one of four enemy fighters that flew over the bay. Trailing smoke and flame, the plane glided into the side of the ammunition ship *Lewis Dyche,* anchored a quarter mile from the two PTs.

The ship exploded with a roar, taking her 71 merchant sailors to the bottom with her and lifting the PTs out of the water. The concussion badly damaged the boat hulls; two PT sailors were killed and ten men wounded by the blast and falling debris. It was the last visit of the *kamikazes* to Mindoro, but a spectacular one.

As Commander Jannotta said in his report: "This new weapon employed by the enemy – the suicide diver or human torpedo – constitutes a serious threat to naval forces and to shipping."

The Mindoro PTs won a Navy Unit Commendation which read:

> As the only naval force present after retirement of the invasion convoy, this task unit served as the major obstruction to enemy counterlandings from nearby Luzon, Panay, and Palawan, and bore the brunt of concentrated hostile air attacks through a five-day period, providing the only antiaircraft protection available for persons ashore. The gallant officers and men . . . maintained a vigilant watch by night and stood out into the open waters close to base by day to fight off repeated Japanese bombing, strafing, and suicide attacks, expending in three days the ammunition which had been expected to last approximately three weeks in the destruction or damaging of a large percentage of attacking planes.

When fighter planes began to fly in Mindoro, Americans went ashore on Luzon. Some hard fighting remained, but the war was nearing the end.

The last two PTs lost in the war were, sadly enough, victims of their own mates.

During the landings at Nasugbu, in western Luzon, on the night of January 31st, ships of the screen were attacked by twenty or more Japanese midget submarines. One of the little craft sank the PC 1129. Immediately afterward the destroyer escort *Lough* attacked a swarm of thirty or more *kamikaze* explosive boats. Naturally the screen vessels were nervous about small vessels in those waters.

On the following night, Lieut. John H. Stillman set out to hunt the suicide flotillas with PTs 77 and 79. (The 77 had already been treated roughly by friendlies; it was the boat damaged by American Army bombers during the repulse of Admiral Kimura's bombardment flotilla.)

Lieut. Stillman's orders were to stay south of Talim Point, because the American destroyers were patrolling north of there. While the PTs were still three miles south of Talim Point – well within their assigned area – they ran into the destroyer escort *Lough*, the same ship that had shot up the explosive boats the night before, and the destroyer *Conyngham*.

The *Lough* fired starshells and the PTs fled south at high speed, trying to identify themselves by radio and signal light. The destroyers meanwhile were trying to raise the boats by radio but failed. They did not see the PT light signals.

The PTs still might have escaped, but hard luck 77 picked that evil moment to run aground. A shell from *Lough* hit her, blowing the crew into the water. The *Lough* shifted fire to 79, and hit her on the portside. The boat exploded and sank, carrying down with her the skipper, Lieut. (jg) Michael A. Haughian, Joseph E. Klesh, MoMM1c, and Vincent A. Berra, QM3c.

The 30 survivors of the two boats, swimming in the light of the burning 77, assembled and held a muster. Besides the three dead on the 79, Lieut. Stillman was missing. He was never seen again.

The shipwrecked sailors swam together to an enemy-held shore two miles away. Guerrillas sheltered them until February 3rd, when they were picked up by PTs 227 and 230.

On March 2, 1945, just two weeks short of three years after he left the Rock on Lieut. Bulkeley's PT, General MacArthur landed on recaptured Corregidor. Finally, he had returned. And he returned the same way he had left – by PT 373.

In the last days of the war, the PTs fought the familiar kind of mop-up action against bypassed pockets of Japanese troops that they had been fighting for three years in the Pacific. Nightly patrols fought minor actions, but targets became harder and harder to find. When the war ended on August 14, 1945, the Japanese came out of the woods and the PTs learned for the first time the tremendous enemy power they had kept bottled up far from the fighting front.

At Halmahera, for instance, six PTs picked up Lieut. General Ishii, Commanding General of the army forces there, and Captain Fujita, Naval Commander, and took them to 93rd Division headquarters on Morotai, where they surrendered 37,000 troops, 4,000 Japanese civilians, 19,000 rifles, 900 cannon, 600 machine guns, and a mountain of miscellaneous supplies.

For almost a year the PTs of Morotai – down to two understaffed squadrons at the end – had held at bay a Japanese force powerful enough, in the days of Japanese glory, to conquer whole nations and to hold vast stretches of conquered lands in iron control.

The Japanese themselves paid the top tribute to the PT fleet. "The enemy has used PT boats aggressively," one of their tactical publications read. "On their account our naval ships have had many a bitter pill to swallow."

So much for the past of the torpedo boat. What about its future?

The PT fleet was quickly disbanded after the war. Today, although the Soviet navy has more than 500 motor torpedo boats – according to *Jane's Fighting Ships* – and even though Soviet-built torpedo boats ply Cuban waters almost within sight of American shores, the U. S. Navy has not a single PT in commission.

But in the waters of Long Island Sound and

in sheltered bays on the Pacific Coast strange craft are roaring about — experimental craft that lift out of the water to skim along on hydrofoils at dazzling speeds (though even the modern hydrofoil cannot attain the breath-taking speeds ascribed to the PTs by overeager reporters during the days of the MacArthur rescue run).

The Navy is puttering about with these hydrofoils, arming them with homing torpedoes, experimenting with tactics to use against swift nuclear submarines — the capital ships of future navies.

There may again be a job in the Navy for the dashing young sailor who prefers the swift give and take of small-boat service to the staid and plodding duty on ships of the line. There may still be room in America's arsenal for David's giant-killing slingshot.

Appendix 1

Specifications, Armament, and Crew

American PT boats, with only a few exceptions, were of two types, 78-foot Higgins-built boats and 80-foot Elcos. Draft to the tips of propellers was five feet six inches. Power supply was from three Packard V-12 engines giving 4,500 shaft horsepower. Tanks held 3,000 gallons of high-octane gasoline and 200 gallons of potable water. Normal crew was three officers and 14 men, though the complement varied widely under combat conditions. The boat could carry enough provisions for about five days. The boat weighed 121,000 pounds, of which 30,000 were contributed by four torpedoes and tubes, a 40 mm., two twin 50 caliber, and one 20-mm. antiaircraft gun, one 37-mm. cannon, two rocket launchers with eight 5-inch rockets, a 60-mm. mortar, and a smoke-screen generator. In combat, PT skippers often improvised other armaments to adapt to local conditions. Pound for pound, the PT boat was by far the most heavily armed vessel afloat. Top speed under ideal conditions was 43 knots. Conditions were seldom ideal.

Appendix 2

LOSSES SUFFERED BY PT SQUADRONS

Destroyed by surface ships: by gunfire, 5; by ramming, 1 (this one, 109, was destined to become one of the most famous boats of all time, because of the subsequent employment of its skipper, John F. Kennedy).

Destroyed by aircraft: strafing, 1; bombing, 4; *kamikaze*, 2.

Destroyed by shore batteries: 5.

Destroyed by mines: 4.

Damaged by surface ships and beached to prevent capture: 1.

Lost in transit on transports sunk: 2.

Grounded in enemy waters and destroyed to prevent capture: 18.

Destroyed to prevent capture: 3 (the boats left behind by Lt. Bulkeley's squadron on quitting the Philippines).

Destroyed by U. S. aircraft: 3; by Australian aircraft, 2.

Destroyed by surface friendlies: 2.

Destroyed possibly by enemy shore battery, possibly by friendly destroyer: 1.

Lost in storms: 5.

Destroyed by fire and explosion in port: 6.

Destroyed in collision: 3.

Total: 69.

Appendix 3

Decorations Won by PT Sailors

Congressional Medal of Honor: 2.
Navy Cross: 19, plus two Oak Leaf Clusters.
Distinguished Service Medal: 1.
Distinguished Service Cross, Army, with Oak Leaf Cluster: 1.
Distinguished Service Cross, Army: 2.
Distinguished Service Medal, Army: 1.
Silver Star with Oak Leaf Cluster: 30.
Silver Star: 342.
Legion of Merit, Degree of Officer: 1.
Legion of Merit with Gold Star: 2.
Legion of Merit: 29.
Navy and Marine Corps: 57 (including one awarded to John F. Kennedy).
Bronze Star with Gold Star: 4.
Bronze Star: 383.
Commendation Ribbon with Gold Star: 3.
Commendation Ribbon: 120.
Distinguished Conduct Star, Philippines Government: 4.
Distinguished Service Cross, British: 6.
Distinguished Service Medal, British: 2.